AF594714

Praise for *Notes of an Aging Pervert*

A meaningful, beautiful and necessary book on how to get old. Being slutty and being alive for a long time is a true honor and a privilege. This book lays it all out in frank and profound terms. I loved it. Let's get old together and truly live it and not lose any of the things we used to be but just do them all better.

Margaret Cho

I owe a debt to Janet Hardy for her work as a kink writer. Her words helped me write about my own life as a pervert. All who think and write about the joys of the body cannot help but think about its briefness, its limitations, and the pain of its upkeep. Hardy has written a personable, lighthearted, and honest foray into territory most people fear and yet everyone, if they are lucky, must face: getting old. She writes with bravery, a chuckle, and not an ounce of self-pity in what can best be described as a series of glimpses — at her life, her body, and her many loves as someone over sixty-five, the "boundary between adulthood and so-called old age," in her words. I can't say I fear ageing less after reading this book, but I hope I get there, and I hope I have someone like Janet holding my hand every step of the way. This book is that hand-hold for hedonists, and we are lucky to have it.

Alexander Cheves

Radical transparency is a rare thing. Throughout this book Hardy tears away the veneer so many of use to cover up the bumpy nature of our internal lives. As a person of iconic stature within sexual and relationship communities, Hardy bravely exposes the deep intimacies of her life to reflect on the personal experience of getting older and how that affects her current perspective on living a meaningful life. This book is superb, which is no surprise since it emanates from the mind of one of the queer community's most interesting thinkers and writers. Each second of our existence we get older. All of us. Everyone must ultimately wrestle with the realities of aging and its impact on sex, relationships, and more. This book will help its readers to age with the grace and wisdom Hardy so eloquently offers us.

Race Bannon

Notes of an Aging Pervert

Notes of an Aging Pervert

Janet W. Hardy

UNBOUND EDITION PRESS

Atlanta

Some parts of this book appeared in a different form in *Reed Magazine,* under the title "Witnessing."

Most of the people mentioned in this book appear under their own names, but in a few cases I have changed names and identifying details upon request.

Similarly, some of the illustrations were drawn directly from people I care about; others are composites of the aging perverts I've known, loved and / or admired from a distance through the years. The ones drawn from actual individuals are labeled with names.

Thanks to all of you, known, anonymous, and composite, for inspiring this book.

FIRST EDITION

Printed in the United States of America

LIBRARY OF CONGRESS RECORD

Name: Hardy, Janet W., 1955 — author.
Title: Notes of an Aging Pervert / Janet Hardy.
Edition: First edition.
Published: Atlanta : Unbound Edition Press, 2023.

LCCN: 2023935041
LCCN Permalink: https://lccn.loc.gov/2023935041
ISBN: 979-8-9870199-6-2 (fine softcover)

Designed by Eleanor Safe and Joseph Floresca
Printed by Bookmobile, Minneapolis, MN
Distributed by Itasca Books

123456789

Unbound Edition Press
1270 Caroline Street, Suite D120
Box 448
Atlanta, GA 30307

This book is dedicated to Edward,
who is Charley to my Rosie and vice versa.

Contents

1. On Me 19

2. On Pain 29

3. On Appearances 39

4. On Strategies 47

5. On Setting an Example 57

6. On Hurrying 65

7. On Appearances, II 89

8. On Remembering 97

9. On Loss 103

10. On Transitions 113

11. On the End 121

Notes of an Aging Pervert

1. On Me

I used to teach classes in what kinky folks call "pain processing." The concept will be familiar to anyone who has taken classes in the Lamaze Method, or in many kinds of yoga or martial arts: it's about divorcing pain from all the feelings that usually accompany it, such as fear, anger or worry — which is to say that you clear your mind of the past and the future, staying doggedly in the now. In the now, you may find that the pain itself is manageable, or perhaps even pleasant.

Of course, I was teaching these techniques to rooms full of sadomasochists who wanted to know how to play harder and longer, so my perspective may be a little, well, perverted.

But the basic skills are easy enough to learn. There are some physical tricks with breath and visualization, but those are just ways to keep you in the moment instead of rocketing forward into the future ("How long is this going to go on? I don't think I can stand it") or backward into the past ("Why is this happening to me? What did I do wrong?"). I can teach you how to do it in an hour or two, but it will take you a lifetime to master it — and some sensations will always be bigger than your ability to process them.

Later, when I started teaching classes about polyamory and other forms of consensual nonmonogamy, I found that my advice about painful feelings like jealousy, displacement, or insecurity sounded familiar: stay present in the moment, don't distract yourself with imagining what you "should" feel, just let the feeling run through you and see what can be learned from it. You don't have to be a big pervert like me to do this: pain processing, whether physical or emotional, is useful in nearly every part of life.

But all my techniques and practices fall short when I think about my own aging, and especially about its inevitable endpoint — which is to say, death. That may be one sensation that's too big for me to process.

+ + +

Before we move on, I should introduce myself. If we've met (on the page or in person), feel free to skip this part — but if we haven't, this book might confuse you a bit.

I'm sixty-eight, the parent of two sons and a stepdaughter, all grown. My first grandchild joined the world last year. Notice that I'm not mentioning my gender. I think the label that fits me best — if I must use one at all — is "gender-irrelevant," in that not one of the things I do these days has anything to do with my gender. My birth certificate, for whatever that's worth, says "female." I live with my male-bodied, equally genderbent spouse in Eugene, Oregon.

This is something like my thirteenth or fourteenth or maybe twentieth book, depending on how you tally second and third editions. The one most everybody recognizes is *The Ethical Slut,* a guide to the principles and practices of, well, being a happy and considerate slut. *Slut* was cowritten with my dear friend and co-conspirator Dossie Easton, and has succeeded beyond our wildest dreams. Less popular but still reasonably successful are a bunch of books — both solo and collaborative — I've written and occasionally illustrated about other alternative sexualities. As a result, I've traveled the world teaching about sex, kink, genderqueerness, and general sluttery, and appeared in TV, radio, documentary films, and a million or two podcasts.

Until a decade or two ago, I practiced what I preached, and had friends, lovers, and play partners all over the world. (When you're the visiting expert, a whole lot of people want to play with you, and who was I to say no?) While I'm not doing that anymore, for reasons I'll get into, those years of sluthood taught me more than you could imagine about friendship, about love, about pain, about ecstasy, and about where all those experiences intersect — a nexus which I like to call my life.

+++

Sixty-five is the commonly accepted boundary between adulthood and so-called "old age," and it's the age when many people choose to retire, if they can, from the work they do for a living. The year I turned sixty-five was the year I retired from the small publisher of books about alternative sexualities that I'd founded and run since 1992. Earlier that year, a couple of my relatives had died and left me money. I didn't need to run the publishing company anymore, and I was glad to be done with it: It had devoured my life and several of my relationships for the better part of thirty years, and I was over all that. (And, yes, I know how incredibly lucky those unexpected windfalls make me. After a lifetime as a freelance editor / small publisher, I fully expected to be arguing with book printers from the nursing home.)

I am not done, however, with being a writer and educator about polyamory, BDSM, genderqueerness, and all the other phenomena that get shorthanded as "alt-sex." I stopped having alt-sex, or for that matter sex in general, quite a few years ago. But for someone like me, who's been steeping like a very happy teabag in various forms of pervery for decades, alt-sex becomes a lot more than what you do in bed: It's a paradigm, a way to think about things that, on the surface, have nothing to do with sex or romance or relationships. Like, for example, aging.

The problem with a word like "aging" is the same as the problem with a word like "pain" — it doesn't have a solid definition; it varies by mood, circumstance and intent. We use the same word to describe the sparkly heat of a well-administered spanking that we do to describe a stubbed toe or an amputation, which causes a lot of confusion for those who can't comprehend why anyone would ever seek out such an experience. And we use the same word to describe the graceful, decades-long accumulation of love and wisdom that we use for the hateful calcification of body and mind, the slow downward spiral that has only one endpoint.

We have the blunt Anglo-Saxon "old," the piss-elegant "elderly," the alarming "geriatric," the respectful if slightly sycophantic "venerable," as well as the sociological "senior citizen," and a bunch of abominations like "seventy years young," "spry," and "in one's golden years." I often call myself "old" simply to get used to the sound of the word in my mouth; I'm not old compared to some people, but I'm old as hell compared to others, and that's not a situation that will reverse as the years stream by.

I suppose if you take it completely literally, aging is what happens when you're stuck in linear time, which I usually am. From the very first sentence of his masterpiece, *Slaughterhouse-Five,* Kurt Vonnegut tells us that his protagonist Billy Pilgrim "has come unstuck in time": Sometimes Billy is an old man, but then his consciousness suddenly awakens in infancy, or as a young soldier during the firebombing of Dresden, or in early parenthood, or on his deathbed. So that's what life might be like if you could unmoor yourself from the linear progression of seconds and minutes and hours and days and years and decades and all that. I think I'd prefer it to the tedious one-way march during which I'm writing this book.

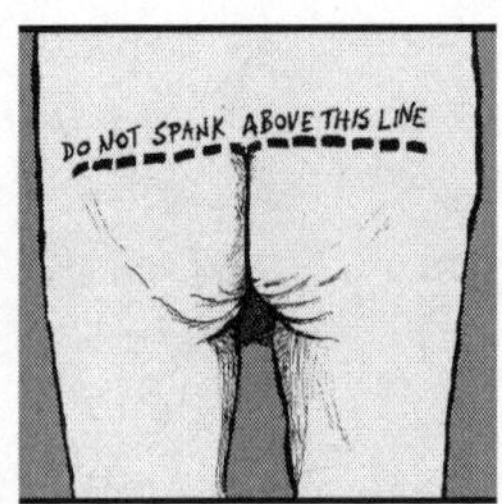

The thing is, my years of being a pervert — a term I prefer to the clinical "sadomasochist" or the winky "kinkster" or the protocol-laden “leatherwoman” — have come close to unmooring me from that river, at least on occasion. Although I started out as a top (terminology borrowed from gay men’s sex, meaning the doer or penetrator), I soon discovered that bottoming to intense sensation gave me these amazing moments of being utterly in my body, unable to imagine anyplace but where I was or any feeling but what I was feeling: I couldn’t remember the past and I didn’t care about the future. (The great paradox, of course, is that being utterly in one’s body short-circuits the intellect, so the spirit flies, free of time and space.) Later, I started being able to get there while topping, and later yet, while doing nothing erotic or sexual at all.

But the thing about those ecstatic moments of total presence and acceptance is that as soon as you think “Wow, I’m really in the moment,” you’re not in the moment anymore. *(Goddammit.)* Newborns can do it, I suppose, but nobody who’s been on the planet for more than a day or two can remain in that state of consciousness for more than the blink of an eye: Living in time and space requires remembering the past and anticipating the future.

What a bore.

At the ice cream store yesterday, the counter was staffed by one man, past middle age, who explained that his helper was running late.

As he handed me my dish of Jamoca with caramel sauce, he told me the price, and then looked at me and backtracked: “Unless you’re over sixty-five?”

"I'm sixty-eight," I told him.

"We're the same age, then."

I chuckled. "It's not a bad age, is it?"

He hesitated. And then I really looked at him. His shoulders were hunched in a way that suggested a neurological or bone disease that almost had to be painful. His t-shirt was stretched at the neck and dirty. Did he really want to be working at a Baskin-Robbins at our age?

It's easy for me to forget that a healthy and well-to-do sixty-eight represents a dizzying amount of privilege: an affluent family, a lifetime of competent medical care, an almost complete absence of trauma, and a heaping helping of plain old dumb luck.

I paid for my treat and looked for a tip jar, but there wasn't one. I wish there had been.

✢✢✢

Back in the years when countless gay men were being felled by an insidious and malignant disease, I noticed that some of my friends were facing something that most of us wouldn't have to confront until decades later: their own mortality. Many held the hands of their friends and lovers who were facing the inexorable ticking away of their last minutes. Many others were no longer alive to do so.

I don't think queerness and death had been tied together in quite that way until then, but I think they are now, in a lot of complex and important ways. Queers had already learned that they weren't entitled to a lot of the good stuff that got handed out to straights (jobs, marriages, life without lies), but the AIDS plague was when

they learned that they might not even be entitled to their next several decades. Not that any of us are entitled to those, but few must confront their potential absence so early in our lives.

Some gay friends in my age cohort somehow survived those years. From the outside, they seem to be living the lives of most sixtysomethings: Some are single and some married; some are sexually active and others are done with the whole thing; some still engage in a busy schedule of teaching and activism while others have retired to the country to spend their remaining days hoeing weeds and feeding chickens. But I don't think a single one of them takes his life for granted.

Nothing in my own life has ever made me confront my own mortality in that way: Aside from the typical tweaks and owies of living in an aging body, I am absurdly healthy. And by the time I became the busy slut I was for three decades (after, believe it or not, a decade and a half of hetero vanilla monogamy), the world had already figured out what kinds of sexual practices could introduce a killer virus into one's system. So I simply didn't do those things (none of which were integral to my sexual response — yet another way in which I am incredibly fortunate). I worried a bit about herpes and chlamydia and all that, but I never really worried about HIV and I still don't.

Somehow, though, perhaps by osmosis, I think the queer way of confronting mortality seeped into my bloodstream years ago, and will swish around my circulatory system every minute of however many years I have left.

Of course, as I write this book, we're in what we fervently hope to be the waning days of another pandemic — COVID-19. I can't speak for any others of my queer cohort, but I don't worry overmuch about this one either, at least as far as my own health is concerned. I obey the rules to protect the people around me, many of whom are far more vulnerable than I, but so far, my usual combination of unearned confidence and plain old dumb luck has gotten me through.

And honestly: if I die, I die.

2. On Pain

My sister, bless her, once said: "I thought I was ready for getting older. I was expecting the wrinkles and the loose skin and the gray hair. But nobody told me it was going to *hurt.*"

You said it, Sis. Even those who are fortunate enough to age "gracefully" will admit that some measure of pain — from a mild nag in a joint to an unignorable blast down a nerve — comes along with the extra time on the meter.

I'm no exception. But in the last year or two, I finally began to pay attention to the throng of doctors, nurses, articles in the paper, webpages, friends, and strangers telling me that frequent aerobic exercise helps with pain. I loathe exercise, but I splurged on a fancy rowing machine, attached an arm to it for my iPad, and chose a favorite TV show that I am not allowed to watch if my ass is not seated on the machine. I could in principle just sit on the seat and see who's fucking whom on *Our Flag Means Death,* but that's not all that comfortable, so once I'm on there I might as well row.

It's worked remarkably well — I hurt a lot less, and I suddenly have actual shoulders, and muscles in my legs. Also, the hint of a set of abs, which is truly startling. The chronic backaches that bedeviled me for decades are almost gone, and even the Evil Hip is restricting its wickedness to one or two nights a week instead of constant lightning bolts. (Both hips are actually Evil. They take turns torturing me; the left one is in the ascendant as I write this. Neither of them pays attention to safewords because they are Evil and do not believe in consent.) But my hands and feet are arthritic and getting worse, and no exercise machine in the world is going to fix that.

+++

The great irony in all this, of course, is that I spent more than three decades of my life chasing after pain.

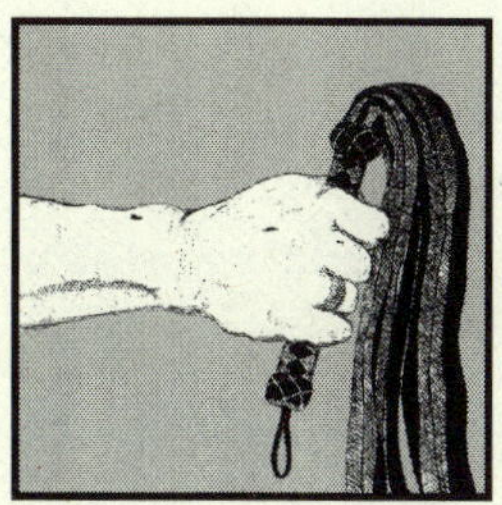

Looking back at those years, I don't think it was so much the actual pain I was after as it was the catharsis. I grew up in the kind of household where voices were rarely raised, physical contact was avoided except under the most formalized of circumstances, and arguments happened behind closed doors. My mom told me once that the only time she ever heard her folks fight was when they had an argument about an eggbeater (why would anyone argue about an eggbeater?). It was an ordinary spat of the kind every household sees, but, Mom said, "I was sure it meant they were going to get divorced." My dad's family was even more reticent — as the youngest and most rebellious son of a strict New England household, he was sent away to school at the age of eight, and having known his terrifying parents I have no reason to believe that he was treated affectionately before then.

My folks did an amazing job raising us, given the raw material they had to work with. But emotional expressiveness was simply not in the cards. The threat, "I'll give you something to cry about," which I swore as a child never to say to anybody and haven't, was heard more than once within our walls. I'm guessing my folks learned it from their folks, who learned it from their folks in turn. Small wonder that my fantasies — which date back to my earliest memory — had to do with people being punished to the point of cathartic tears, and comforted by a loving parental figure.

There are, of course, many ways to reach catharsis, and I would go on to explore some of those many years later. But the only path my child-mind knew was extreme pain, so that idea got knitted into my sexuality from its earliest formation.

+++

It's hard to make a convincing argument in favor of pain — except that it's taken me to a lot of places I couldn't have gone on my own.

BDSM, at least the sensation-heavy kind I do, is a practicum in distinguishing between good pain and bad. It looks absurd to an outsider when someone who is getting their back savaged with a bullwhip stops the scene because they have a cramp in their foot. The welts from the whip are a spiritual channel between loving friends, whereas the cramp is unintentional and meaningless, and is moreover a distraction from the party in the back.

Kink has brought a lot of good things into my life, including a career and more dear friendships than I can count. But the ability to stay in good pain, while keeping a feeler out for the bad stuff, might be my favorite. It comes up in everything from massages (I look for professionals who are willing and able to work deep enough to make me scream, and who can tell the difference between the scream and "let's back off that pressure a little bit") to the gym to the dentist's chair and beyond. I have been known to doze off while getting a tooth drilled.

Someone asked me recently if the ability to stay with things that are uncomfortable is also a factor in my emotional life. I wish that I could have assured them, "Absolutely — I'm much better than I used to be at confronting and negotiating conflict." I guess it would be partly true in that I am now able to deal, reluctantly and timidly, with everyday arguments. But to say that my pain processing skills have made me great at conflict would be a lie. I suck at conflict, always have, and all that can be said for my thirty-plus years as a pain player is that I now suck a little bit less than I did when I entered the scene at thirty-five.

Pain is also arguably responsible for my current relationship, which at nearly twenty years is the longest of my lifetime.

When people ask how Edward and I met, the quickest answer is "Which time?" — except that just brings up more questions. Here's a bit more backstory.

I first met Edward at one of the excellent dungeon parties he used to throw. They were held in the basement of a huge old Victorian in a sketchy part of San Francisco, which boasted a

Edward
then + now

backyard hot tub (with illegally high fences so nobody could peek), a fascinating collection of queer and psychedelic art, and, of course, a fully equipped dungeon with various roomlets, niches, and nooks for everything from a medieval rack to a roomful of mattresses for aftercare, along with the usual array of massage tables, bondage crosses, and so on.

The parties were great, especially if you were queer — Edward's social and romantic life has always centered on butch lesbians, butch bisexuals, and a handful of young men who look like butch lesbians. He'd addressed the eternal problem of bad behavior from straight male attendees by doing his best to keep them out: If you were a straight man, you had to attend with a partner, or in drag. (A lot of hetero folks, including me at the time, were less than thrilled with The Edward Solution, but I never heard anybody suggest that there wasn't a problem. I've never encountered a non-gay, publicly sexual environment in which single straight men *weren't* a problem.)

I don't suppose Edward and I had ever said more than the few words required by common courtesy to one another. I thought he was entirely gay — so sue me: The *Desperately Seeking Susan* drag, complete with torn fishnets, a miniskirt, high-heeled boots, safety pins, and leather was my evidence. (He says, "Madonna stole that look from me.") He had the imperious, petulant quality common to many gay men who are in charge of things. And he thought I was entirely hetero, because he'd only seen me with my then-partner, Jay.

In short, we didn't like each other much. That was Meeting #1.

Fast-forward a decade or so. The parties weren't happening anymore, so aside from the occasional polite nod at a community gathering, I had no idea what was happening in Edward's life. He had probably heard about my breakup with Jay, and he'd seen me with enough women by then to know he'd guessed wrong about my orientation, but we moved in different circles and there was no reason for us to interact.

I was living in an industrial loft in Oakland, which left something to be desired in terms of heating and accessibility (the elevator was constantly out of order, and the loft was on the fourth floor), but was great for play parties. At one of them, I was seriously annoyed by the number of guests who either no-showed after RSVPing, or never bothered to RSVP and showed up anyway — and I noticed that the offenders were nearly universally under forty-five.

I'd been scanning the personals for a while, but in a fit of pique after everyone went home, I changed my search criteria to five years older than they'd been. Immediately, this ad popped up in my notifications:

> *Bi genderbent male in early 50s, looking for play partners and maybe more. I've mostly been dating men for a while, so I'm hankering for a woman, but I'm most strongly attracted to butch women. Ideally I'd like a nurturing top, maybe someone who has raised kids ...*

and so on. Honestly, my first thought was that one of my friends was pranking me. But I figured there was no harm in answering, so I did.

It took us a couple of rounds of correspondence before each of us started to figure out who the other one was. At that point, all our mutual acquaintances — of whom there were many; the Bay Area kink scene is not as large as you might think — started getting phone calls from both of us, each trying to learn more about the other.

So we met for coffee. And he was nothing like the queen bitch I thought I knew.

"I had to give up doing the parties," he told me. "Years ago, I was on the wrong side of an auto-versus-pedestrian crash. At the time I was told it was almost all soft-tissue injuries, and that nobody knew whether they'd be a problem later on. Well, they turned out to be a problem."

I learned that he was in pain nearly all the time, that he spent most of his hours horizontal, and that his doctors had told him that he could expect to live a pretty good life... for a man twenty years older than his chronological age. (At this point I'd say it's closer to ten years than twenty, but there's no question that he lives the life of a much older person.)

But the other thing I learned was that dealing with pain and disability had taught him presence and patience. "I can't change any of this," he said, "so I've had to learn to give in to it." Pain had turned the imperious queen into a meditative, thoughtful man. Of course, the imperious queen still makes the occasional appearance: In my experience, it's possible to learn new ways of being, but not eliminate the old ones. I've gotten way better at not being the manipulative nurturer that was my default for many years, but she still puts in the occasional appearance as well.

Edward moved in with me later that year, because he was spending so little time in his city apartment that the roaches were pretty much running the place and were considering signing the lease. We got married a year or so later, so that I could add him to my health insurance policy. That meant he could see my doctor, who had been a good friend to both of us for years, and he could add some of the expensive but effective drugs for nerve pain to his existing regimen of opioids and cannabis. The meds helped, and so did sleeping on a decent mattress, eating fresh food, and the rest of the habits that can ameliorate chronic pain.

Our pairing left a lot of people confused, though. Despite my relationships with Dossie and a few other well-known women, I was never really welcomed in the lesbian community — until Edward and I became a couple. I think the underlying logic was something like, "Well, everybody knows that Edward only dates dykes" — but whatever the logic, suddenly I was family. And when we ran into an old friend we hadn't seen for a decade or so and told her about our marriage, she looked gobsmacked for a moment and then blurted, "That's the queerest thing I've ever heard!"

And, yeah, it kind of is. I only recently ran across the term "queerplatonic" (the lingo of alt-sex changes faster than even I can keep up with it, and it's my *job*), and had a jolt of recognition.

Edward and I haven't had sex or kink together since our honeymoon eighteen years ago — our relationship is still open in principle, but neither of us has felt the need to look for sex or play partners in ages, although I'll still play with one or two longtime friends if we happen to be in the same city. In lieu of sex, we work on our house, hang out with each other's kids, and take care of each other, just like other couples our age.

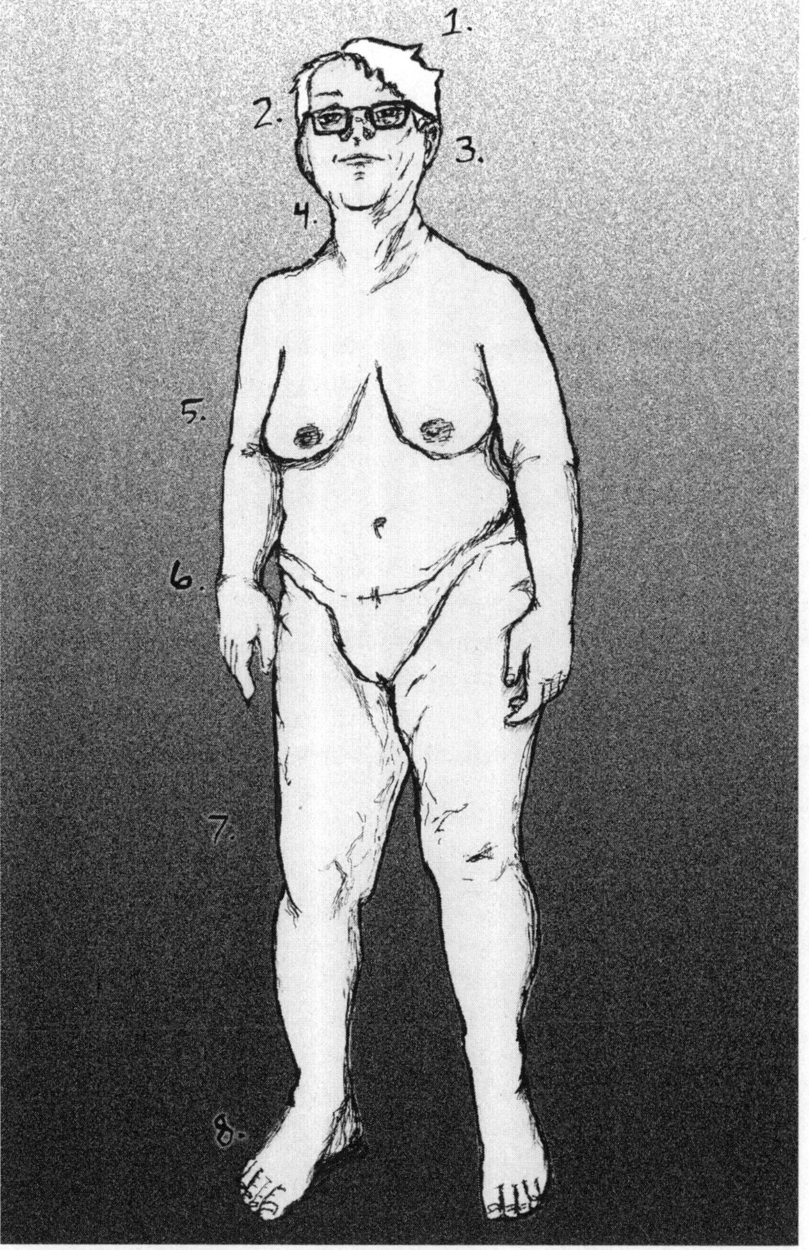
1.
2.
3.
4.
5.
6.
7.
8.

3. On Appearances

I'd like to say that the appearance part of aging — the loose skin, the saggy muscles, the gradual merger of boobs and waistline — doesn't bother me. But you wouldn't believe me, and I wouldn't believe me either. Few adults can live in our appearance-obsessed culture and not have occasional moments of mourning for what came before.

In the interests of preserving the past, I asked Edward to take the reference photo for this drawing a couple of weeks ago. If you've been trying to imagine what someone who's led a life like mine must look like, here's your answer.

1. My head is pretty much the only place on me where there's still an appreciable amount of hair. (I haven't shaved my legs or pits in a decade, and if you're more than two feet away from me you'll never notice.) I bleached it platinum for quite a few years, and frequently overlaid it with pale silvery violet; in my youth, old ladies frequently dyed their hair pink or pale blue or another pastel hue, so I figured mine was "ironic lavender."

   But then there was a month where the roots got a little overgrown, and I noticed that most of them were as white as the hairs I was trying to lighten, so I just shaved the whole mess off and let it grow back in. And, miracle of miracles, the follicles had learned how to be white: My hair was a gorgeous silver that was way better than any of the colors (my native mud-brown, auburn, chestnut, dark blond, lavender, aqua, pink — well, you get the idea) I'd spent time and money creating through the years.

There are times when I miss looking like the first crocus of spring, but I don't miss it enough to go through all that again.

By the way, I think everyone should shave their head at least once in a lifetime. It's a great way to discover that the world doesn't end when your hair goes away. And once you know that, you can feel free to try any weird-ass cut or color or other experiment, because if it all goes to hell, your razor is waiting patiently for your return.

2. When I was young and trying to build my career as an advertising copywriter, I wore glasses with plain glass in them, figuring they added a few years to my age, and made me look serious and knowledgeable. And I discovered that I *love* wearing glasses. They're a built-in fidget — pushing them up my nose, looking over them for emphasis, taking them off and gesturing with them. Who needs smoking when you have glasses? Years later, of course, I started needing them for real. Of course, by then I had those extra years, and I *was* serious and knowledgeable.

   My eye doctor says that the cataracts in both eyes are getting close to needing removal. And apparently these days, when you have cataract surgery, you can pay to have lenses implanted that correct whatever other problems the eyes might have. I am amblyopic — the vision in my right eye puts me right on the edge of legal blindness, and is not correctable with normal lenses — and I'm fascinated by the idea of having binocular vision for the first time in my life. I once sat through *Captain Eo,* the Michael Jackson music video that debuted modern 3D technology and that you could only see at Disney parks, four or five times in a single day: I was able to see depth, or a simulacrum of depth, for the first time, and I was captivated.

I suspect that it's too late for an artificial lens to make any real difference to my depth perception or my coordination; I've long since learned to compensate as best I can for my deficits in those areas. (Hint: If something is coming toward you, look at it, look away for a moment, then look back, and project from there. I'm not sure it's learnable past a certain age, and it doesn't work when something is coming straight at you, as my dismal history with all ball sports will attest.) But I'm still looking forward to finding out what it's like having two working eyes.

On the other hand, they will pry my beloved specs from my cold dead hand, and I'm not sure how to explain that to the enthusiastic young we-can-fix-your-eyes-so-you'll-never-need-glasses-again ophthalmologist.

3. I didn't notice until I started to draw that this pose is very typical of me: I'm looking down my nose, just a little bit. I think it's a combination of wanting to look taller and wanting to reduce my inventory of chins. A voice teacher once showed me how that posture was tightening my voice and reducing its volume, leading to poor projection

and a lot of sore throats. I've worked on straightening my head, using the usual imagery of a string reaching from its crown into the sky, and sometimes I even succeed. But anytime I'm feeling self-conscious — like, for example, being photographed in the nude — back it goes again.

4. This is probably one of the most expensive mouths you've ever encountered. I must have been eight or nine when the dentist discovered twelve cavities since my previous appointment, and for years that was pretty much typical, with the usual ritual of being shamed for my dilatory brushing habits.

 Then, in my twenties, I was told that the problem was actually that I had a significant overbite and an underdeveloped lower mandible, and that all my back teeth were being ground away. (Fuck you, kid-shaming dentist, wherever you are.)

 My husband and I — respectively, at the time, a junior engineer and a clerical employee who did some writing whenever she could talk her employer into letting her — couldn't really afford the next few years: six teeth pulled, two years of braces, major surgery to break and reposition both my upper and lower jaws, two months with my teeth wired shut, and another six months of braces. I can't remember what it all cost except that it was a lot. I'm told the surgery is now done with plates, and requires no hospital stay and no wiring-shut, and I have very mixed feelings about that. But since then I've had only the usual number of cavities, and my smile and my profile are a lot better.

I do take some pride in the fact that I interviewed for, and got, my first corporate writing job while my mouth was still wired shut. I'd practiced for several weeks by reading road signs as I drove, learning to use my lips and tongue for the clearest diction I could manage: I sounded like those silver-spoon Ivy League graduates for whom the clenched-teeth diction is a status marker. Apparently after I left the room where I had been interviewed by five people, the head of the company turned to everyone else and said, "I dn't knw abt y gys, bt I'm imprssd."

5. Say goodbye to these, my friends: as I write this, they are moldering in someone's medical waste bin. I was warned to prepare myself for some grieving, but, honestly, I did that years ago — when the high, full breasts I once loved became a pair of empty envelopes nearing my navel. They've been gone for exactly one month today. I recently spent a delighted day trying on all my shirts, and every single one of them looked better.

I'd spent years threatening my tits: "One, just one, cancer cell, and you guys are *toast.*" And then I had more money than I needed, and I realized I didn't have to wait for my visit from the Cancer Fairy.

When I approached my androgyny-loving spouse Edward about the prospect of top surgery, he shrugged: "My friend Carol had it, and she was much happier afterward." (As opposed to the time early in our relationship, when I told him I was thinking of growing my hair out, and he yelped like he'd been tasered.) Nobody else seemed to be able to think of a good reason to keep them, so I found a doctor and got the process started.

I'm planning a bra-burning party for a day that Oregon is out of fire danger. After all these years, I will finally get to be an actual bra-burning feminist.

6. You might not be able to tell from this drawing, but the long scar that looks like the top elastic of a pair of underpants is in fact the remnant of an abdominoplasty (people call it a "tummy tuck," but *ewww*) to repair the damage to my abs from two c-sections. The tiny vertical mark at its midpoint is the last vestige of the cesarean scar; it matches the tiny vertical mark directly below, the cleavage of my outer labia: One mark for things coming out, and another for things going in.

   With the matching scar across my chest, I now look like I'm meant to be folded in thirds, like a letter.

7. I wasn't sure that I'd be able to render cellulite in pen and ink, but apparently I can.

8. As I age, my feet remain one of my few vanities. I did my time as an advertising copywriter wearing three-inch heels and pantyhose, but I don't think I've worn a pair of heels or anything with pointed toes in thirty years, and it shows. When I sit at the nail salon with all the ladies getting pedicures, I notice that their feet are broken in all sorts of ways — bunions, corns, crossed and deformed toes, all the ills of the contemporary mutilation known as "fashion." I spread my strong, straight toes and smile smugly to myself.

That said, my arches are not all they could be. According to my doctor, fat women should not dance barefoot.

The dance was worth it. Maybe the heels would have been too.

4. On Strategies

It's modish these days to talk about "future me" — the time I will spend on my rowing machine tonight, for example, is a gift to "future me." It's actually not a bad paradigm for thinking about self-care. But the hard part is imagining what "future me" will be like, and what she will want to do with what remains of her life.

In the centuries before you and I were born, people learned how to get old by watching the people around them getting old: Their grandparents and great-grandparents, their aunts and uncles and cousins, their neighbors and acquaintances, and, of course, their parents.

But few of us these days live in environments where we can spend time with people who are much older than us. Even our media serve us up a feast of information about the young, and very little about the inner lives of the over-sixty.

When I look around me, though, I see a range of approaches to aging. At one extreme, you spend your last few decades eating broiled chicken breasts and kale salad, taking brisk walks with weights attached to your limbs, and dressing in snazzy size-small tennis whites. At the other, you stock your kitchen with brownies and booze and excellent cheese, think of walking as the thing you do to get from your car into the supermarket, and boast a closet full of caftans and comfortable flats.

My first serious encounter with "future me" took place, like most of my epiphanies, in the dungeon of a playmate. (He was a type I've come to recognize: a terrific top, whose life outside the dungeon was a bit more of a train wreck than I could deal with on a regular basis. When I remember him, I think about the many folks who have rejected me because I am "too sane," and I can see their point; the boundarylessness that makes a person flounder in the real world often makes for terrific sex.)

He had bound me face-out to a sturdy St. Andrew's Cross, and was happily engaged in putting vicious little clamps all over my belly and breasts and thighs, leaving them there long enough for the sensation to start to ebb, and then yanking them all off.

While I used to be a fairly stellar impact bottom, I was no better than most folks at dealing with non-impact sensation — and the leathery skin I'd built up on my ass was doing me no good at all on my tits and belly. Every one of several dozen clamps had bitten like a wild creature as it went on, settled into an increasingly gentle squeeze, and then stung like death as it came off. I was shrieking — lord, how I love to shriek. And in the middle of one shriek, I came unstuck in time.

The fortysomething body that was bound to the cross — plump and with stretch marks, but still supple-skinned and resilient — suddenly became the body of a woman in her sixties, past menopause and creaky, with a headful of gray hair and a snatchful of very little hair at all. And that old woman's immediate response to finding herself in that place at that time was to burst into hysterical tears.

Fortunately, my chosen tormentor was a writer too, because he didn't hesitate when, between sobs, I gasped, "Do ... you ... have ... a pad

… and a pen?" (Few tops would have greeted my request with such unquestioning aplomb.) He unbound me, bundled me into a soft, pink quilt, put me to bed, and went and got the requested items.

He wasn't the kind of guy who takes a hysterical bottom into his arms and soothes her back to base level, and I'd known that when I'd first asked him to play some months before. But as I scrawled out a core dump of my feelings, he tiptoed back into the bedroom to hand me a glass of ice water and a china cup full of chocolate chips. It will help you understand why I was seeing that guy when I tell you that the chocolate chips were cold from the freezer, and that he himself didn't eat sugar: He was keeping the chocolate for me, for exactly such a situation. This made me cry harder but didn't keep me from writing the piece.

By the time I was done, I was back to my fortysomething self, and the marks on my front were mostly faded away. We hugged goodbye and I went home.

Here is what I wrote:

> *This is a simulated emergency. This is a drill. A simulated individual is trapped within a collapsed simulated structure. We have a report of smoke rising from structure. It is unclear whether smoke is simulated or real. Repeat, status of smoke unconfirmed. Do you copy?*

Simulated individual is singing. Repeat, singing. We believe the song to be a showtune, possibly early Sondheim. This is a drill.

Simulated individual is uncertain whether collapsed structure is physical or a construct of individual's endorphin-soaked brain. Simulated individual has been told that structural collapse is inevitable, even if simulated. Team is uncertain whether structural collapse is current or imminent. Repeat, team uncertain of temporal placement of simulated structural collapse. Do you copy?

This is Red Team notifying Blue Team that simulated individual lay awake last night awaiting structural collapse. Simulated individual dozed and dreamed of real emergencies. Simulated individual awoke torn between fear and relief. Simulated individual resorted to unsimulated self-abuse. We have a possible source for smoke. Repeat, a possible source for smoke.

Technical team has been dispatched to ascertain likelihood of structural collapse. Technical team is entering structure. Alert all stations: technical team fears imminent structural collapse, possibly simulated, but technical team is taking no chances. Technical team is going to lunch. Can technical team bring you anything? A cheeseburger and a Coke? Medium well, right?

Alert all teams: focal point of structural collapse indeterminate, possibly bone, possibly brain. No personnel are to enter structure. No, we have no address, stupid, this is a simulated structure. Repeat, no personnel are to enter structure. Simulated individual is so fucking tough, let her figure it out for herself.

Alert! Alert! Smoke has increased. Visibility poor. Smoke may not in fact be smoke. Junior here says it smells like plaster dust. Junior, are you sure? Damn, I can't see a fucking thing.

This is a simulated emergency. This is a drill. Repeat, this is a drill. Do you copy?

Simulated individual remains within simulated collapsing structure. Simulated individual is open to other options. Lots of luck, simulated individual. Simulated individual dreams it all backwards. Simulated individual is taller and thinner. Simulated individual is practicing writing her name in different ways. Cancel alert. Repeat, cancel alert. Individual may or may not be simulated. Do you copy?

Smoke appears to be sound of possibly simulated individual's name broken down into vibrating molecules. Smoke appears to be individual's bones, ground to powder, drifting. Smoke is dissipating. Smoke is gone. Repeat, smoke is gone.

This has been a test. Had this been a genuine emergency, you would have been asked to give a damn. Did someone say something about a cheeseburger? Do you copy? Do you copy?

+++

It's a little opaque, I know. When you're unstuck in time, a linear narrative is too much to expect.

+++

I complained once to my friend Paul about ads targeted toward seniors, with their endless stock photos of smiling, slim, white people with perfect teeth and tans and immaculately styled hair, often hiking, golfing or swimming. "To read these magazines," I whined, "you'd think that there was no other way to get old."

"You just need a different role model," he told me. "How about Quentin Crisp?"

I've seldom had my brain reset so dramatically. Crisp, for those not fortunate enough to have yet discovered him, was a beautifully effeminate gay man from an era when being out as a "pansy" often led to jail and / or assault. His memoir, *The Naked Civil Servant* — about his years working as an artist's model in early twentieth-century London — is a testament to a life lived without apology. I cannot begin to imagine Crisp in tennis whites. Yet he lived to the substantial age of ninety-one and gained a worldwide reputation as a raconteur and cultural critic — activities that require little or no kale salad.

On the other hand: about a year ago, I had a series of severe chest pains. Their etiology did not show up on the MRI, the stress test, the x-ray, or anything else we tried. The cardiologist shook his head with frustration. Eventually, for lack of a better idea, he suggested an angiogram, although none of his tests had indicated that any of my blood vessels were seriously clogged.

Much to everybody's surprise, the pains turned out to come from a relatively minor blockage in the circumflex artery, the one doctors call the "widow-maker." He Roto-Rootered it out, stuck a stent in there, and that was the end of the chest pains.

What I haven't been able to find out — and, believe me, I've tried — is whether that now makes me a heart patient, or whether my symptoms were from a rare one-off called "variant angina," which has very little to do with arterial blockage. The rows of prescriptions on my bureau last year argue for the former, but my doctor is cautiously eliminating one after another from my regimen, and the chest pains have not recurred.

If I were as blasé about dying as I've made it sound, I'd have gone on taking care of my body as if I planned to live forever, blithely overconsuming steaks and brownies and potato chips, and letting the exercise equipment downstairs gather dust. And if that regimen simply meant that one day soon I was going to grasp my chest, make a strangled noise, and keel over dead, I think I'd be okay with that.

What worries me much, much more is the possibility of a slow, downward slide, losing one ability after another — body and brain shutting incrementally down, until I am the kind of old lady who sits in a recliner and watches television all day, with the path to the end barely distinguishable from the end.

So I've been trying to learn how to take care of Old Janet's body. After a lifetime of shameless hedonism, I'll probably never learn to love a green salad as much as I love warm crusty bread dripping in pungent olive oil. And, so far, I've had no luck at all finding a form of exercise that I'd do even if it weren't good for me. But life in Old Janet's body is at least tolerable, and I think I'll be able to go on doing this as long as I think it's doing me any good.

When I look for role models for how to manage this process, though, I get confused. My mother was very much of the brownies-and-steaks school of thought. (I still have certain foods I think of as "Susan Hardy Memorial Foods." They include ice cream sodas, overly cheesy pasta dishes, and Panettone at Christmastime, with a thick layer of butter.) Hers was a lifetime spent struggling with her weight — her parents had tormented her daily for her barely plump teenaged figure. To her dying day, she never again ate grapefruit, dry toast or soft-boiled eggs, because she'd been made to have them all, unseasoned, for breakfast every day. Aside from the occasional and short-lived "diet," she spent the rest of her life eating what she wanted. And then the chronic cough she'd had for years began to act up, so that was an excellent excuse to avoid exercise (not that she'd ever needed an excuse). By the time the cough developed into chronic obstructive pulmonary disease (COPD), she was more or less immobile.

Late in the progress of her illness, her doctor prescribed a diuretic to offset the edema in her legs and feet, and she discovered to her delight that it had completely killed her appetite. When I flew down to help with things she could no longer do around the house, I discovered that she was living on one Skinny Cow diet ice cream bar for breakfast, and a few bites of whatever she'd made her husband for dinner. Her skin was hanging on her newly gaunt frame like a de-tumescing hot-air balloon.

(That was the visit when Mom greeted me at breakfast saying, "I woke up this morning feeling so *happy!*"

Given that she was getting sicker by the day, this seemed odd. I asked, "How come?"

"I realized — I don't have to do any Christmas shopping this year!"

As an example of finding the positive in death, this is hard to beat.)

When I suggested that perhaps such a rapid weight loss was not in the best interest of her health, she set her jaw and said, firmly, "I intend to die at my goal weight." And she did, a few months later, almost certainly sooner than she would have if she'd maintained her lean body mass.

It was her choice, and I genuinely believe that other people's health choices are not my business — but it still makes me both furious and sad that even when confronting death, she still hung onto that lifelong desire to be slim and pretty.

On the other hand: my father, who had never reconciled himself to Mom's weight, took as his second wife a longtime Weight Watchers instructor. The two of them led an abstemious lifestyle of little to no sugar, a minimum of fat and refined carbs, and daily long walks around their home on an island in Puget Sound. His wife died of cancer at about the same age that my mother had.

After Mona's death, Dad read her diaries and learned for the first time that she lived in daily terror of getting fat, because she was afraid he wouldn't love her anymore. He felt awful to think she'd believed his love was that conditional; he'd loved her very deeply. Once she was gone, it took him (a decade older) less than a year to follow her.

Dad was diagnosed with the same cancer that had killed his wife — pancreatic cancer, an increasingly common killer. His Parkinson's Disease, previously well controlled, flared up during his period of grief. He arranged his own death, with the help of Washington's very humane death-with-dignity laws. The interesting part to me is that even after he set his departure date, his refrigerator was still stocked with skim milk and grapefruit and thin-sliced bread.

Yes, my mom's last years were less active than my dad's — the COPD had her more or less chair-bound. But when I put all those lovely ice cream sodas and bowls of pasta and slices of bread-and-butter on one side of the scale, and a few more years of healthy mobility on the other, which way does it tip?

5. On Setting an Example

As you can probably tell, I'm kind of confused about how to grow old — but I know how to die, because my father taught me. And since you'll never get to meet my dad, this will give you an idea of who we're talking about here.

After it was all over and the guys from the mortuary had come and gone, my sister Leah suddenly said, "Where's his wallet?"

We looked everywhere: in the room downstairs he'd moved to, in his real bedroom upstairs, under the bed, in the closet, in the mudroom. No wallet.

"You don't suppose ... he had it in his pocket?" I asked dubiously.

And that's exactly where it was. A woman from the mortuary called us back the next morning to say that there had been, not one, but two wallets in his pockets: one, with cash, in the front pocket; one, with credit cards, in the back.

Dad had awakened that Sunday morning, knowing he was going to die that afternoon, and dressed carefully in his uniform of khakis, a polo shirt, a v-necked cashmere sweater, and his wallets. Because God forbid he should die in his pajamas, or that someone could come to the door wanting to get paid for delivering the newspaper and he wouldn't have his wallet on him. The largest concession he was willing to make was to remove his watch and leave it on the nightstand, and to take off his father's handsome jade ring, which never left his finger, and hand it to my sister. Beyond that, death found him neatly dressed, hair combed, beard trimmed, and with both wallets where they belonged. The law calls it "Death With Dignity," which in his case was great marketing.

+++

It was late on a Sunday afternoon in January. The others in attendance — Dad's dear friend Anne, whose credentials as a nurse meant we didn't have to have a stranger in the room; Anne's husband Tim, looking a bit queasy; and Leah — were planning a final toast with and to him, as he waited for the lethal draft to take hold.

I was not going to participate in the toast. Not because I loathe scotch, although I do. But I'd anticipated this moment, and when I'd left my home in Eugene to drive up to Dad's place outside Seattle, I'd packed a bottle of excellent rum specifically for this moment.

However, the last stop I'd made in Eugene was at our neighborhood cannabis dispensary. "I'd like some of the Siskiyou FECO," I told the young man behind the counter. (For those of you not fortunate enough to live in a state with liberal cannabis laws, FECO is full-extract cannabis oil, a tarry black substance to be taken one drop at a time. I called it my "black tar weed.")

"Oh, I'm sorry, we're out of the Siskiyou," he told me. "But we have some other FECOs that are pretty similar." He brought one out and showed it to me.

"Sure, that'll be fine." I paid for my purchase and hit the road.

Of course, because pain is a contrary motherfucker, I felt okay that night, despite the long drive. Dad and I sat together at his counter, eating the spaghetti I'd thrown together from what I'd been able to find in his pantry and freezer. Afterward, we did possibly the strangest thing either of us had ever done: We went through the obituary I'd written at his request. He asked for a shift in tone, an addition to his list of close friends, and the correction of a minor factual error. I suppose you could look at it as writing the resumé for his next job — but as strange as it was for me, it must have been absolutely surreal for him.

I asked how he was feeling. "Okay. Scared," he said, which broke my heart a little.

"You know you don't have to do it tomorrow if you're not ready," I said. "Nobody would think less of you."

"I know," he said, with some effort. "But I'm as ready as I'll get."

"Are you in pain?" The last time I'd asked, the answer was "no."

"Yes," he said.

"Then I guess it's time," I said, and changed the subject.

+++

Early the next afternoon, my back decided it was unhappy with the way I was handling tension, and staged a small rebellion. I squirted a tiny amount of the FECO onto a cracker and ate it.

Anne and Tim arrived shortly thereafter. As we chatted, I noticed an odd, warm, dry feeling in my eyeballs. My vision tracked in jerky silent-movie-like bursts. My heart sank.

"Shit," I hissed to Leah. "That stuff had a lot more THC than they told me. I am fucked up."

She looked at me helplessly: The last thing this scene needed was one of its principals in a significantly altered state of consciousness. "Maybe if you had a drink, that would relax you?"

I shook my head. "That just makes it worse." (I'd learned this the hard way the last time I'd had a glass of wine on top of my usual dosage.)

We looked at each other. Neither of us had a clue. "I'll have a glass of milk," I decided. I had no reason to suppose that milk would help, but I figured it couldn't hurt.

Anne was in Dad's room, "making the bed," by which she meant putting down disposable underpads: Dad's greatest fear about having Leah and me in the room was that it would be "messy." We pointed out that we had both had babies, and that was pretty messy too, and he should decide what he wanted instead of trying to anticipate what we wanted. Amazingly enough, he believed us, and agreed that we could be there.

+++

The law in Washington is very specific about how a chosen death should work. Two doctors must agree, two weeks apart, that the patient's readiness to die is reasonable. They sign some paperwork, and then one of them orders a prescription for a powder that is chemically very similar to the injection used in veterinary euthanasia. (The powder, I learned, cost around $2,000. What. The. Fuck.) The patient himself must pour the powder into the glass, but someone else can add the water or juice into what is apparently a truly foul-tasting concoction.

So the scene was this: Leah, Tim and I were sitting around the guest-room bed. Anne, for whom this was not her first rodeo, steadied

Dad's Parkinsonian hands so he could pour his powder, and topped it up with some orange juice. He chugged it down like a pro, and made a wry face while Anne was taking the glass of dregs away and replacing it with a heavy crystal tumbler.

Leah poured everyone but me a hefty Scotch as I sat helplessly, waiting to toast him with the last inch of milk in my glass. I was uncharacteristically quiet, because I was afraid that anything I said would come out weird — or at least weirder than sitting in a corner nursing a glass of milk while the source of half my DNA was confronting his final journey.

We clinked glasses and drank. Leah poured a second round. By the time the level in his glass was near the bottom, Dad was fading out.

"Someone should take his glass away," Anne said quietly. I was closest, so I went over and took it out of his hands — I had to pry his fingers gently away, one by one.

He opened his eyes briefly, smiled, and said, "Good idea." Those were his last words. I was the last one to touch him.

And then we waited.

I thought longingly of the speed and finality that was euthanizing a pet. When someone dies in the movies, it goes one of two ways: Either they close their eyes and that means they're dead, or they slump over with their eyes wide open. This was a longer and less conclusive process by far.

Dad's eyelids fell till a new-moon crescent of milky white was all that showed. His mouth did something similar — with no muscle tension to pull it upward, his lower lip fell away from his bottom teeth. And perhaps if you've attended many deaths, this is not news to you, but to me it was a revelation, the first of several.

I could not take my eyes away from him — my stoned soul was mesmerized by the process revealing itself to me.

As I watched, his face began to morph. First it was a skull. Then the face of an ape. Then the face of an angel. Then it was my dad, my Daddy, my father. And then a skull again... and the process repeated itself, around and around and around.

And then, during an angel phase, I saw a disturbance — a ripple in the air, like the ripples rising from a hot highway, over his left shoulder. The morphing stopped.

He was gone.

And I was so glad I knew it, because the next few hours started off excruciating and evolved into low comedy, as the rough involuntary breaths that novelists call the "death rattle" continued at longer and longer intervals.

Toward the end, we'd all be certain it was over, and Anne would be on her feet to take his pulse so she could declare the time of death, and the rest of us would rise to leave so she could do her job ... and then his body would clatter like a Model T and we'd all sit back down.

Toward the end, we — three tipsy people and one stoned one — were finding it darkly hilarious; there were several fits of contagious giggles. But with a couple of years of hindsight, I don't think that was inappropriate: The body's determination to hang onto the spark of life despite its occupant's desires is the oldest, darkest and funniest joke on earth.

The next time I saw my sister was a month later, at a small memorial gathering. In a moment of privacy, I said, "I've been thinking about Dad's death." (I'd already told her about my hallucinatory experiences.) "Was it transcendent for you too, or was it just because I was stoned?"

"It was perfect," she said.

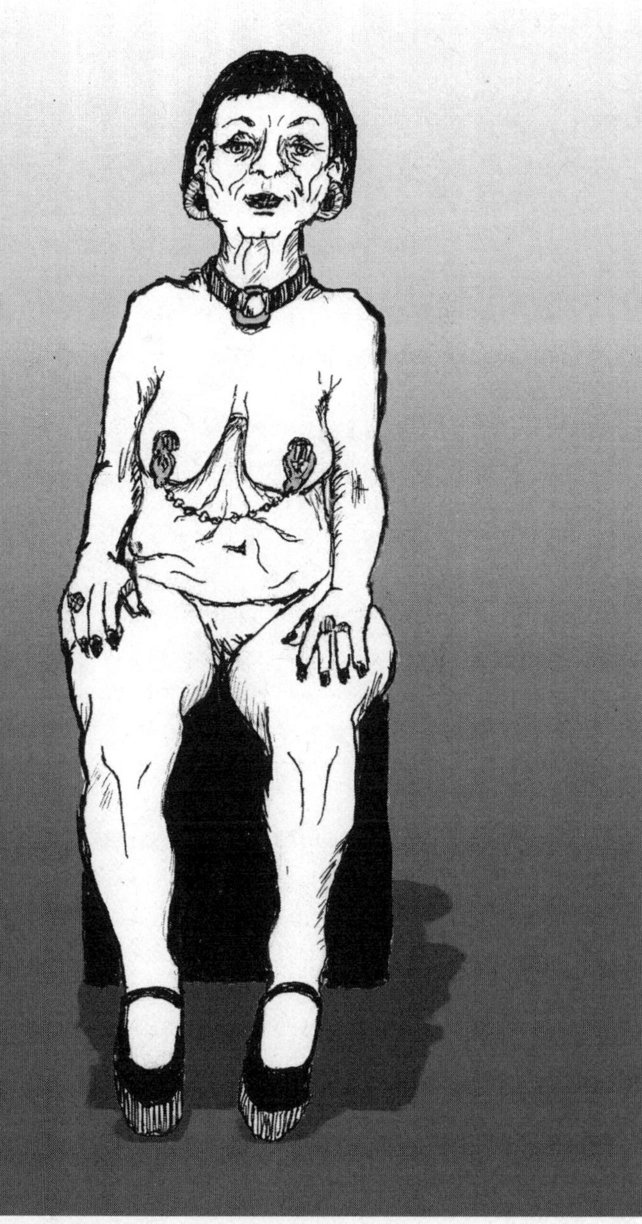

6. On Hurrying

Edward recently started looking into what might be involved in moving to a retirement community. My feelings about this are mixed: On one hand, he really does need more support than I can easily give him; on the other, I keep imagining spending the rest of my life hanging out with my parents' friends. (Nothing against my parents' friends — they're great people. They're just, you know, *old*.)

As I look back over my life, though, I see a pattern: I've always been in such a hurry, and I don't know why. If I were a cop, I'd pull me over and ask, "Hey, lady, where's the fire?"

I was never much good at being a child. I was one of those pudgy, bookish children who enjoys the company of adults more than that of other kids, because adults talk about more interesting stuff. In grade school, my classmates considered me an expert on all matters sexual. I wasn't — I remember being profoundly startled at around eleven years old to discover that men peed and came out of the same hole, which still seems a little weird to me. But they sensed that sex was important to me and that I was someday, when my body and the law permitted exploration, going to know a hell of a lot about it.

Adults often saw me as one of them. I have a clear memory from eighth grade of a group of teachers on smoke break calling, "Hey, Janet, come up here and amuse us for a while!" Even then I thought this odd (though flattering); now I consider it downright strange and kind of creepy. But I joined them and amused them for a bit, and got a small, desperately desired taste of adulthood.

By high school I was charging forward as fast as my miniskirted legs would carry me. Of course, most teenagers long for the trappings of adulthood – but I look back now, and for the life of me I'm not sure what I was in such a rush to grab. A lot of it, I think, had to do with sussing out the limits of my ability to control my environment: Sexy clothes, for example, give their wearer a kind of power that to a sixteen-year-old is intoxicating.

(At my twentieth high school reunion, I chatted for a while with a man who had been in several of my classes but whom I'd never known well. "I've always wanted to ask you something," he said. "Back then, when you didn't wear a bra and people could see your nipples through your shirt, did you know what you were doing?"

And I couldn't answer him. Did I wake up that day and think, "Today is my day to torture a bunch of horny teenaged boys?" No. But did I notice that wearing that shirt got me attention? Yeah, probably. And that's being a teenaged girl in a nutshell.)

Of course, what I wanted most desperately of all was a boyfriend.

I can't remember ever feeling in those days what I now know to be sexual attraction toward a boy, or for that matter a girl. I was having near-constant fantasies about spanking and discipline, but they never included genital sex – so I didn't recognize them as sex fantasies, and thus made no attempt to reconcile those impossible desires with what I thought was "normal" sexuality. Wanting to kiss, to make out, to have intercourse – I don't think I ever once got turned on by those thoughts, although the desire to do those things was urgent and real.

My high school crush was an amazing overachiever, who simultaneously maintained the school's highest GPA, was a starter on the basketball team, and played the piano beautifully. I often imagined kissing him, but when I tried to find a turn-on in the fantasy, I came up, well, dry. The crush was real and hopeless and painful, and half a century later I have no idea what it was I wanted so badly.

I can guess, though. In high school I skated between cliques — not pretty (or, let's face it, normal) enough to be popular; too socially awkward to be a slut (I would have been if anybody had thought to ask, but nobody did); too mouthy to be one of the quiet kids who wander like Hollywood extras through the halls of every high school; not coordinated enough to be a jock; not science-y enough to be a geek; too much of a good girl to be welcomed among the stoners. But having such an exemplary boyfriend would have cemented me a place in the hierarchy. It would have gotten me seen. And god, did I yearn to be seen.

As things stood, though, I had no solid place in the social life of a high school student.

I figured everything would be better once I was in college. So I went to summer school, did some independent study, and graduated a year early.

And there it is again, the huge rush forward. The question is: What wisdom did I miss in my frantic stampede toward my future? Some things people learn in high school — quadratic equations, the Bill of Rights, what a topic sentence is — are easy. But then there's the harder stuff: How do you take care of yourself? Is altering your consciousness a good idea, and, if so, how do you want to do it, and how often should you do it, and how can you make sure it causes as little harm as possible to the rest of your life? What kind of adult do you intend to be? Is sex something that you want in and of itself, or are you trying to gain status, build your reputation, avoid teasing or bullying, get a boyfriend or girlfriend, attain power? How will you find friends in an environment where you aren't seeing the same people five days a week for nine months?

I missed all that, and I paid for it, and sometimes I still do.

+++

The tiny detail I'd left out of my headlong rush into the future was that most people go to college to learn things. I'd imagined skimming along on a frothy mixture of Cliff's Notes and bullshit, which had worked fine till then — but the professors at UC Santa Cruz were not so easily dazzled. Much of the campus was accessible only on foot, by bike, or via a system of trams I never really got the hang of. I hated long walks, especially on hills, and hadn't ridden a bicycle since I was twelve. Hence, I missed more classes than I attended. I also found myself unable to perform many of the functions of adulthood — things like keeping my room in a manageable state (I drove away my roommate and nobody else wanted me, so I had a double room, piled high with papers, dirty clothes and art supplies, to myself), finding new friends, or managing the small allowance my folks sent me every month.

It's easier to figure out what I missed from college: everything. I was attending an excellent school at its academic peak. I thought I had nothing to learn from my professors, or from anyone: I was in college because going to college was what smart people did, and I was quite sure I was too smart to learn anything from anyone else. I wrote reams of mediocre poetry (and ignored any input from instructors or workshop members — I don't think I ever wrote a second draft of anything), took a few art classes, barely finished the required courses for humanities majors, moped around, and smoked a lot of weed.

Thinking back to those days makes me want to kick my college self squarely in her perky young ass.

I didn't flunk out, although I should have. But when I realized that more of my energy and social life were going into my part-time job as a movie "usherette" than into all my classes put together, I began to think about better uses of my time.

By that point I'd met Frank (who would go on to be my doggedly vanilla first husband and the father of our kids) and lived with him for a year, so when he moved back to Davis, his hometown, I followed him. I invited him to get married, and we did, when I was twenty and he was twenty-one.

I was a fucking adult, goddammit, and getting married was what adults did.

+++

I did eventually go back to school, at UC Davis — taking the bare minimum of courses necessary to finish my bachelor's degree. But then I had a few days when I felt kind of queasy, and then my boobs got tender, and, well, I think you can guess the rest of that story.

It was actually Frank's and my second pregnancy — the first one had been when we were still in Santa Cruz. But even my desire to race forward toward whatever came next was not enough to convince me that a baby at nineteen was a good idea. With my folks' help, I'd had an abortion (this was in the days when they were only legal if you could get a doctor to say that it would be dangerous to your mental or physical health to have a baby) and got on with my life.

But two years later I was pregnant again — I guess some people just shouldn't have IUDs — and by then we were married, so, what the hell, we had Miles, and I was a mom at twenty-two. That's not all that old by the standards of the generation before mine (my mom had me at twenty), but it's still pretty damn young.

The world these days is complicated enough that it takes at least a couple of decades to get the hang of it. At twenty-two, I could hold down a minimum-wage job setting type for the local paper, prepare an edible meal, do laundry if nobody was too picky about getting it folded and put away, and keep house well enough that nobody was going to die of toxic fumes or spoiled food. Frank was at about the same level, so between the two of us we maintained a rathole apartment, took care of our pets, and occasionally ate something besides ramen and peanut butter.

Having a child, though, required a whole different level of functioning. Miles was the easiest of babies, but even an easy baby is a little tornado of needs requiring everything you have to offer: your boobs and your lap and your sleep and your budget and your tear ducts. But I was determined to live an unchanged life, as women did before concepts like "confinement" entered the language. If I'd been a hunter / gatherer, I told myself, I'd have given birth, gotten up with my newborn baby in my arms, left the placenta for predators, and kept on hunting and gathering. I picked up my newborn and rushed once again into my future.

I suppose most every new parent feels trapped to some degree — but I wonder whether some of the wisdom about being a single woman that I'd blithely avoided might have made things a little easier. (Certainly, knowing that there was such a thing as BDSM, and that it was something people like me could do, would have prevented *so* many mistakes.)

When Miles was about four, Frank and I decided to order takeout pizza for dinner, because neither of us had the energy to cook. I picked up my bag and keys to go to the car. "I wanna go!" Miles whined.

"I need some time by myself," I told him. "I'll only be gone for a little while."

His enormous brown eyes welled up. "If you want to be by yourself, why do you have a Miles? Why do you have a Frank?"

That conversation took place more than forty years ago, and it still pierces me to the heart.

+++

By the time I was thirty, I'd figured out that my spanking and discipline fantasies were, in fact, sex fantasies. (I'm very smart in a lot of ways, but not so smart in others.) And Miles's question — "Why do you have a Miles? Why do you have a Frank?" — was echoing in my brain, along with its later addendum, "Why do you have a Ben?" And I didn't have an answer except that I loved them all immeasurably.

But the obvious next step — "How do I get to have a Frank and a Miles and a Ben, but still search out the ecstatic intensity my life is so profoundly lacking?" — was not so simple. I tried with Frank, but his obvious disinterest was a buzzkill for both of us. I tried with other guys I'd met through their personal ads, trying to figure out whether sadomasochism was an itch that would heal after a couple of cathartic scratches.

It wasn't.

In the end, I lost my Frank but kept my Miles and my Ben. Many newly minted perverts are not so fortunate.

+++

When I came of age in the early 1970s, acid was as omnipresent and almost as easily obtained as weed. But the whole idea scared me: A deep dive into my own brain, I suspected, would dredge up all kinds of stuff that I wasn't ready to acknowledge. Coming from my repressed, upper-middle-class background, I had no sense of my brain and body having anything to do with one another (even now, I find the idea of bondage counterintuitive — you mean if you can restrain a person's body, you can restrain their mind too?!). I still liked weed, but eventually turned away from it because the munchies were so severe and irresistible that I could easily imagine doubling my weight if I kept it up: The day I was heating my lunch, couldn't wait, and wound up chugging maple syrup straight from the jug, was the end of my career as a stoner.

Booze has never really been my thing either. I've always suspected that I'm a much better person after one drink, no more and no less, but I've never figured out a way to stay one-drink tipsy.

Which is to say that by the time I started my life as a pervert, I was starved for ecstasy — for a path out of all the hard work of thinking, a controllable way to achieve an altered state of consciousness.

Remember, my fantasies were and are about catharsis. When I was exclusively a top, I had no idea that kink could take me there — and I wasn't self-aware enough (or unselfconscious enough) to tell my partners that I needed them to cry and beg. So it was only when I began to bottom that I started to recognize the ecstatic potential of bottoming to heavy pain.

A memory from around 1991, when I was just beginning to experiment with the business end of the riding crop:

> I'm lying face down on the bed. He's caning me, going a bit faster than I can manage with my breath and muscles. I start to wail and beg; there may have been a bit of thrashing as well. The caning does not stop. Somewhere through the cloud of

endorphins, I think: *Well, I've tried begging and I've tried thrashing and it didn't make this stop ... So why bother?* I go utterly quiet, feeling the blows but not feeling any need to do anything about them ... and I go flying, zooming around the corners of the room and looking down admiringly at my welted ass, for the first time of many.

That first experience resembled my fantasies of resistance and punishment only on the surface, but I learned early on that resistance and punishment were extremely tricky to enact. (In thirty-plus years as an active practitioner, I can count the scenes that met that desire on one hand — either someone falls too deeply into the fantasy of being "bad" and feels awful, or someone gets angry in a real-world way. Either outcome is not fun, at least for me.)

Failing that, catharsis worked fine.

Having tasted ecstatic kink, I wanted more of it — a lot more. My then-partner Jay and I had by that time become moderately famous in the world of community-based BDSM (we'd written at least one well-received book each, back in the pre-Internet days when there was almost no information in print about the whys and hows of kink), and we were being invited to speak at quite a few of the leather conferences that were then springing into existence as a gathering place for pervs of all backgrounds, kinks and orientations. And the thing about what one friend calls “the leather rubber chicken circuit” is that while you’re in a strange city, you meet new people, and you play with them.

It may seem a contradiction: I learned from playing with strangers that love is essential to any successful kink scene. Which is not to say that those one-off scenes were bad (some were, most weren’t). The corollary to my theory is that love happens in odd places — sometimes in a dungeon in a strange city, with someone you’ll never see again.

I became dependent on my ecstasy fix. If a week or two went by in which I hadn’t done a good hard scene, my brain got sluggish, and my usual solutions to issues in my life and work were no longer available to me. By then I was starting to catch on to the brain / body connection — as I said earlier, I’m pretty smart in some ways, but kind of stupid in others. My partner started referring to the sessions in which I bottomed to him as “defragging your brain,” and that was exactly the way it felt. (For those who have never heard of defragging, it’s a way of clearing your computer by throwing out unnecessary stuff and arranging all the information in tidy patterns. Most computers don’t need to be defragged anymore, but it’s still a good analogy.)

By then, Dossie and I had done four books together: *The Bottoming Book, The Topping Book* (which in later editions became

The New Bottoming Book and *The New Topping Book*), *The Ethical Slut*, and *When Someone You Love Is Kinky*. Had we run out of things to write about? Hell, no. Given that we were both on journeys to explore dungeon-based ecstasy, we decided to spend a couple of years in an immersive plunge, exploring everything we knew or could learn about transcendent experience during BDSM, to somehow be turned into a book called *Radical Ecstasy*.

We started playing more than we ever had before (which, when you stop to think about it, is pretty impressive), both together and with others, and journaling about our thoughts and experiences. And we started learning about other people's ecstasies: books by neurologists and researchers, memoirs by our kinky brethren — anything we could get our hands on. The piles of paper rose higher and higher.

And one day, Dossie said over lunch, "I've been thinking maybe we should take a tantra class together."

A word about tantra as it's practiced in such classes: It has very little to do with classical tantra (it's more accurate to refer to it as "western neotantra"), and a lot to do with sex and connection. Its genesis in the US goes back to the Guru Bhagwan Shree Rajneesh, later known as Oshō; you can trace the lineage from any of the major American tantra instructors back to Oshō and his teaching. What it felt like to me was lessons in how to take the arousal that you normally feel in your genitals, and use breath and movement to pump it out all the way to your fingers and toes — filling yourself and your partner with an electricity-like energy, and generating an orgasmic overload that spills out as you moan, wail, and shake.

Of course, Dossie and I already knew how to have whole-body orgasms — we'd been doing it in the dungeon for decades. But when the opportunity came to learn how to do it even bigger and better and faster, we were right there, checkbooks in hand.

Here's the thing about tantra and BDSM and meditation and pagan ritual and prayer and so on: We're all climbing the mountain, but we're climbing up different sides. The peak of the mountain is the few moments you get to be utterly present and in utter acceptance, and your spirit explodes out of you and fills the universe. It's worth a lot of work and pain to get there, however briefly.

We struck lucky, at least at first, with our choice of instructors and environments. Many tantra teachers use a very gendered framework for their instruction: It's all about manifesting your god or goddess energy — and guess which genders get which energy? We wouldn't have put up with that for longer than it took us to find our car keys. But our instructor was a woman who preferred to teach women, so our first several journeys were among people of genders like ours.

At the climax of each weekend workshop, though, everybody attended an afternoon "puja," a ritual in which we all gathered to breathe and connect in pairs and groups. The dress code for the puja read, "Wear whatever makes you feel like a goddess." Given that I have never owned such a garment and never expect to, I went to my first one naked — hey, if I'm a goddess, I don't need clothes, right? By the next time, they'd made a no-nudity rule (gosh, thanks), so I bought some Wonder Woman underpants at Hot Topic and made do.

The goddess thing, along with the droning music, were pretty good indicators of everything I disliked about tantra. But it was a way to move faster and farther into ecstasy, so I wrote off the cultural dissonance and learned what I was there to learn.

I did learn a lot, although perhaps not the things they'd tried to teach me. My favorite part is that every class started with a warning that went something like this:

> *As we practice together, you may find that you're having a feeling like you're falling in love with your partner. The reason it feels that way is that you are, but not in the way we've all been taught about love — the kind that means dates and going steady and living together and getting married. Instead, you're loving the energy of the universe as it manifests through your partner, and they're falling in love with the same thing about you. Please accept the love you find here as something that happens in the moment and don't try to futurize it into something you need to do anything about.*

That's advice that has stood me in good stead ever since: When you embark on a voyage of ecstasy, loving your fellow travelers is part of the experience, and doesn't have to mean anything more than exactly what it is. (Although I didn't recognize it at the time, I think this is one of the fundamental tenets of queerness.)

Unfortunately, most tantra teachers have little or no experience on the dark side of the mountain. These days there are exceptions, but in most tantra environments, practices like kink and gender-bending are frowned upon. Thus, our teacher had no idea that those of us who were longtime kink practitioners were seasoned mountain-climbers — we were considered beginners, albeit surprisingly talented ones.

I'd like to think that disconnect was the primary cause of what happened next, although I suspect our instructor's antipathy toward kinky, butch-ish, mouthy, goddess-averse me may have played a role as well. Whatever the cause, here's what happened.

It was Saturday evening, the last exercise of the day, after we'd all been pairing up with other women for exercises ranging from basic tantra breath-and-undulation stuff through consciousness exercises like telling your partner the things you wish you could say to your mother. We were sweaty and happy and jangling with energy.

"Now reconnect with your first partner of the day," the instructor said. Dossie and I floated over to each other and plopped down on the floor in yabyum position, where each person kind of sits in the other one's lap. "There's no particular instruction for this exercise," the instructor told us. "Just connect through the breath and gaze, and undulate."

Dossie and I got busy doing what we knew how to do, and the energy went off the charts almost immediately. Our mouths met and we began sharing breath, where each of us would exhale into the other one's mouth and then receive the breath in return. I felt a storm rising up my spine ...

Dossie + me

… and in the next moment I began to tip backward. With Dossie riding across my hips, unable to get clear in time, I arched up like a dying bug, our combined weight borne only on my head and feet. (If you offered me a million dollars to do that right now, I wouldn't be able to.) My fists started pounding the floor. I began to scream, and kept screaming uncontrollably as the power surged through me.

My intellect was still functioning, but it became small, distant, and helpless. It told me that what I was feeling was dangerous — that if it went on, I would hurt my body or my brain or both. I thought about strokes. I thought about heart attacks. What I couldn't think about was what might happen next, because I didn't know: I'd spent many hours learning how to achieve this ecstasy, but it had never occurred to anyone to talk about how to stop. Maybe when it stopped was when I fainted, or died.

In fact, when it stopped was when it was goddamned ready to stop. The muscles in my neck and thighs eventually gave out under a combined three-hundred-pounds- plus of completed circuitry, and I collapsed into a little heap.

If you'd asked me at the time, I would have said I was in that exalted and terrifying state for at least ten minutes. Dossie says it was, in fact, a minute and a half, two at most, and I suppose I have to believe her.

Overwhelmed with the memory of terror, I curled up and began to cry. Dossie petted me and reassured me that I wasn't broken, I hadn't done anything wrong, everything was going to be okay. Which turned out to be true, but it took quite a few years to get there.

+++

After the other women in the room had spent a few minutes winding down with hugs and murmurs while I sobbed like a child with a skinned knee, we were all instructed to regather in a puppy pile at the center. Touching other humans when my nerve endings were still raw was the last thing I wanted to do, so this puppy made her own one-person pile in a corner. The instructor — this is the part I have the most trouble forgiving — scolded me back into the pile, and I lay there feeling like I was being sandpapered until it was time to gather our things and go to our motel.

The next morning, Dossie wanted to join the group for the Sunday exercises. She was driving and I had nowhere to go except back, so we went back. When we asked the instructor what I should do about my alarming experience, she said, curtly, "Ground." (Grounding, for those unfamiliar with the terminology, means putting your consciousness into your connection with the ground beneath you and feeling its solidity. It didn't help. In the years to come, it never once helped.)

So I did the Sunday exercises in as low-key a way as I could, pulling my energy into myself instead of sharing it with my partners. And I survived the day, and we headed to our homes.

+++

My instinct, in the wake of that afternoon, was to put away the big hurry and lay as low as I could: no sex, no kink, nothing intense or erotic or, well, ecstatic. Unfortunately, my instinct was overridden by my checkbook. We had a book deadline to meet, and meeting that deadline meant continuing to immerse myself in the world I'd rushed into. We played some more, talked a lot more, wrote a whole lot more. I couldn't give my flayed nerves time to heal — there was work to be done, and we did it, ignoring the fact that I was having frightening bouts of vertigo (I did the final structural edit lying flat on my back while Dossie dictated her input to me, because when I sat up the room started whirling) and Dossie was having regular nightmares. We'd been in a preternaturally open-hearted state for the two-plus years it took us to compile the book, and it turns out that living without a skin has consequences.

Radical Ecstasy was published, and we were and are immensely proud of it, despite it having a smaller audience than almost anything else we've written. But whatever channels had opened in me in that tantra class were not happy about closing. I started having orgasmic experiences every time I took my attention away from my brain and focused on my body. I had an orgasm in an exercise class. I had an orgasm while antiquing. I had an orgasm at the supermarket. And while I was able to conceal what was happening from the people around me (I hope!), that kind of loss of control does not feel good. If you think about the other circumstances in which someone might discover their muscles contracting without volition, you might imagine charley horses, labor pains, heart attacks. It was scary and embarrassing and uncomfortable, and I had no more idea of how to stop than I'd had during the exercise that started it all.

Eventually, it faded. I discovered an ecstatic dance group in my town, which turned out to be the perfect venue for energy practice: I can dance the energy up and down my body. When and only when I'm ready, I allow it to zoom upward and out... and if I do a little private moaning or screaming, the room is full of people and music and shouting, and nobody but me has to know. I can still go back into an orgasmic state at will, but these days I rarely want to.

Remember in the beginning of the book, when I mentioned that I was no longer having sex? Now you know the reason. I still do the very occasional scene when I get a chance to play with one of my old and beloved friends, but I haven't had genital sex in nearly twenty years. There are days now and then when I miss it, but they're rare and easily ignored. I rushed all the way to the end of the line, and I'm pretty sure that journey is over.

And now, in my late sixties, I'm being offered the chance to charge forward once again. Although Edward is only five years older than I, his disabilities add a decade or so to his functional age: living in a seniors' community makes perfect sense for him. Because I want to keep my Edward, it seems I'll have to figure out how to have it make sense for me, too.

For my whole life, a huge part of my identity has been built around being strong and competent. But recently I had to ask Ben to tighten the screws holding down the toilet seat, because my hands are simply not strong enough. The last major household task

I performed, installing some new faucets in the bathroom, left me limping pathetically for several days. I may be competent, but I'm not so strong anymore. What's more, I've become *fragile* — everyday bumps and dings leave big bruises, everyday movements lead to angry tendons and restless muscles, and healing takes weeks or months, not days.

So maybe this move isn't really rushing forward. Maybe it's exactly what I need for the next couple of decades. But I need to spend some time thinking about what wisdom I might be overlooking as I move on.

Which is, I suppose, one of the reasons I'm writing this book.

Rio

7. On Appearances, II

As I look back on a lifetime of fretting over my appearance, I see that I've always been *between* — never pretty, never ugly, always between. When I was young and still figuring out how the world worked, my lack of conventional beauty was a source of angst — I thought, probably correctly, that my looks stood between me and lots of desirable achievements like romance, glamour, and money. But a few decades later, I talk to my friends who were beauties in their day, and they all feel like they've lost something important now that they don't have that attention-getting exterior.

I don't envy them, not anymore. Since the long-ago days when I was desirable purely because I was young, I've always had the choice of being seen or being invisible, by the way I manage my clothing, hair and speech. I love having those options, whereas my formerly pretty friends find that having to work to get attention is a new and unwelcome experience.

What I tell people about my experience of losing weight (which I've done several times, only to gain it back with interest) is that the main difference is that a whole lot of people want to fuck me who I don't want to fuck: In fact, someone who only wants to fuck thin people is exactly the sort of person I will walk several blocks to avoid. I suspect the same is true of being pretty. Make no mistake, fuckability is a kind of currency — but those of us who have never had it have learned to do business in our own currencies of wit, savvy, skill, determination and achievement. And given that these don't go away (barring diseases that affect cognition), they feel like a more stable currency than beauty.

That said, managing one's appearance as the years fly by is still a puzzle. The good part is that invisibility comes easily: If I dress in old-lady clothes, then I'm an old lady and nobody cares what I do. But I think one of the most fundamental human hungers is the need to be *seen* — and that's not always so simple.

There's a wonderful series of photo books of people of advanced years — mostly but not exclusively women — dressed to draw the eye: brilliant colors, flashy jewelry, fuck-you-and-your-age-standards hair colors, all paired with sensibly low but colorful shoes and bird-of-paradise eyeglass frames. I love looking at these photos and fantasizing about dressing like that. But I notice that those folks all live in major cities or in places populated mostly by the retired, where nobody dares point and laugh at the old broad in the orange fishnets. And of course, there's the question of who pays for all that stuff, and how many hours a day one is willing to devote to choosing, curating, and maintaining those gorgeous getups.

But more to the point: When you're old, the line between stylish and absurd gets very iffy. Upright posture and a confident stride will get you only so far (although perhaps further than you'd guess) — but the difference between the lady in the drop-dead ensemble on the book cover, and your tipsy Great-Aunt Mildred who insists on polyester animal prints and refuses to acknowledge that size eight is far behind her, is little but context. And context, as we all know, is everything, especially when it comes to appearance.

I think where a lot of us geezers go wrong is in trying to look younger. That shit never works. Even when your hair is Medium Honey Blonde again, and you've learned how to deal with contact lenses, and you've used all the wrinkle fillers and eye creams your budget permits, something will always give you away — your spotted hands, your scanty brows (or, if you tend toward testosterone, your inch-long Schnauzer brows), the loose skin under your jaw, the dangle under your upper arms that you try not to look at. And somehow, once someone has noticed your secret, your attempts at illusory youth become embarrassing in a way that just giving in and looking old never would.

+++

One of the things I think my gay leather brothers get right, or at least righter than most, is maintaining a culture in which their elders are considered hot. (I love them for this, especially when they post photos of strong, centered, minimally dressed graybeards: I've never found people much younger than me particularly attractive, so those photos take pride of place in my personal fantasy life.)

That's not true in all sectors of gay malehood, but it's true in the one that feels like home to me — the leather/fetish/BDSM community. Leather is the natural home of many men who fall outside what my friend and colleague Midori memorably dubbed "commercial attractiveness," whether by virtue of height, age, weight, or whatever weird criteria the magazines are making up at the time. It's rather soothing to hang out in a world where what you can do with a rope, flogger, or fist is more important than what you look like.

My strong suspicion is that the "bear" and "daddy" aesthetics were born in the days when far too few men got old enough to be daddies, and when the sign of a man in the teeth of AIDS was alarming thinness. I have no idea how to research or prove that question, but my sense of the thing is that these looks cropped up just about the time that people I knew began to die.

(It may or may not be worth mentioning that the other sign of AIDS was the reddish-brown spots of Kaposi's sarcoma. The skin on my arms has gotten so thin, testament to a lifetime of pointedly ignoring anyone who tells me that sunbathing is bad for me, that even a minor impact — like my little dog pawing me for attention — leaves a nearly identical mark. It startles me for a millisecond every time a new one shows up.)

I think the women's community has always offered plenty of options for desirability as well. I've lusted after and played with fat women, skinny women, women older than me, women younger than me, femmes, butches, and women of all colors. And magnetism in that community doesn't seem to change with age: I note that my coauthor and longtime lover Dossie, who is more than a decade older than I, still seems to get laid pretty much whenever she feels like it.

It seems, then, that heterosexuality lies at the heart of ageism, although lord knows other communities (notably non-leather, non-Daddy gay masculinity) are far from immune to it. I suspect such values have their origins in the framing of penis/vagina intercourse, the only potentially reproductive activity that doesn't require external assistance, as the only thing that counts as "real" sex — thus, sex with women only tantalizes if they are, or appear to be, in their childbearing years, and little to no accommodation is made for the realities of aging bodies.

Straight people have a lot of catching up to do. I had lunch with a straight man who was preparing to teach a class to other men about erectile dysfunction, and how to please a woman even if one's dick wouldn't get hard. I sent him a link to some research showing that lesbians — most of whom do not have hard dicks, at least not the built-in kind — report orgasms during sex significantly more often than hetero women. This was news to him.

I could go on forever about the problems of heterosexuality as it's currently enacted throughout my culture. As just one example, if I were to try to untangle the dynamics behind the belief that it is women's obligation to look youthful and pretty for men, I'd have a different book on my hands — one that other people have already written better than I can. And there's another book to be written, in which some brave person tries to tease apart straight men's actual desires from their striving for status: "Trophy" wives and girlfriends are called that for a reason.

And though a fish may not need a bicycle, I do like men, and a distressing number of them seem to be straight.

I once had the opportunity to sit in on a convention of fat women and their admirers. I found that most of the admirers broadcast a weaselly quality that I read as shame plus defensiveness. That was a long time ago, and I think it's a little more socially acceptable these days for a straight man to like his partners well-padded — but many fat women can share stories of men who want to see them only on the sly, because they can't afford the social consequences of being seen with them in public. The same, of course, goes for men who prefer older women.

A handful of straight male celebs appear proudly with a vivacious crone or abundant beauty on their arm, and good for them. But for the most part, any man who wishes to convey his social status chooses the slim young trophy, the golden prize he was told for years was awaiting him when he made it to the big time. One way to look at this is that having a fatter or older girlfriend is like having a boyfriend used to be, but it sucks any way you frame it.

I won't say I've given up entirely on straight men, because I know a few who are miraculously able to rise above all this nonsense. (One good friend of mine honestly doesn't care about his lady friends' size or age; as a result, he dates almost exclusively larger and older women, because there are so many on the market.) But it increasingly seems as though they've given up on me, and I can't say that I mind too much.

As the lines between genders blur — none too soon, if you ask me — it has become more common to see a straight man modeling "feminine" behavior: dressing up as a princess or mermaid to play with a young daughter, vamping for the camera in classic cheesecake poses, rocking a skirt and heels (of the many unfairnesses of the world, the beauty of male legs in heels ranks near the top of my list). A lot of these photos seem to be going for absurdity, but to my eye they are hot, in a way conventional gay-themed drag is not. Such photos telegraph "fearlessness," and I do love a fearless person.

I note, however, that most such men are a generation or two younger than I. For the men I grew up with, the social penalties for female-coded behavior were so draconian that few can escape their iron grip.

A shame. One of the realities of aging is the gradual blurring of secondary sex characteristics: men grow nice little breasts, women's body hair migrates upward to our chins and lips, and bellies sprout with joyous disregard of their owners' genders. Our bodies beg us to gender-bend, but our histories too often shake a stern finger saying "no."

A question to ponder: What will the places where seniors congregate, the residences and nursing homes and community centers, look like when all our body modifications adapt to our rapidly modifying bodies?

I had my first, largest, and best tattoo for my fortieth birthday, a pen and ink drawing of a crescent moon with a woman's face, and stars tangled in her hair. When I described it to the other folks on a computer bulletin board (yeah, this was that long ago), one young man snarked: "Do you know what that's going to look like when you're sixty?"

"Yes," I responded. "Longer."

And here I am, nearing seventy, and it is longer (or was until the boobectomy excised a chunk of it — my tattooist and I are already planning a repair job). And I couldn't care less.

The eleven-strike brand of a stylized elephant on my right calf, which never healed right anyway, is almost invisible now; if you didn't know what it used to be, you'd probably guess that it was the scar from one of those horrible burns folks get from the hot muffler on a motorcycle. And my body has never adapted well to piercings — a piercing in my left nipple stayed tender and weepy for a year and left two visible puckers on either side for decades. The hell with that.

But my other tats still give me great pleasure — the picture and quote from *archy and mehitabel* on my right arm has enabled me to turn many people on to the tremendous and near-forgotten pleasures of Don Marquis, and to greet as a kindred spirit anyone who recognizes it without prompting.

My body is the house I live in, and nobody expects a rambling Victorian, lovely as they may be, to look like a chrome-and-glass condo. I touch up the paint once in a while, keep the vegetation trimmed back, keep the water and power turned on, and ignore the shabbiness that is an inevitable part of structure-plus-time.

And when I find myself living among people my own age, I hope we will all glory in our stretched-out piercings, faded tattoos, and spreading scarifications: We are people with the power and guts to make our bodies look the way we want, and we will wear those emblems with pride all the way to the grave.

8. On Remembering

Something they don't tell you about getting older is that your friends and family get older too, and sometimes they die. And each time someone dies, that's another shared memory blown out like a candle, and your past getting vaguer and vaguer.

+++

I think my mother really started to die when her oldest friend Dot died, a few years before her.

"But you didn't really like Dot all that much, toward the end," I reminded her.

"She'd turned into a real pain in the ass," Mom agreed. Dot had never been a contented person — what made her fun was her vivid, creative, and stylish complaining — but age had withered her wit and all that was left was the bitterness. "But she was the only one who remembered what I used to be like."

Dot and her husband Sam were almost as much a part of my childhood as my own parents. All four were avid card players — bridge, hearts, gin — and my lullaby many nights was the sound of gin-and-tonic-soaked laughter, bickering, point-counting, and bid-reviewing in the brightly lit living room down the hall from my dark bedroom.

When my family moved west in my early teens, we didn't see Dot and Sam for a while. Then Sam died young, Mom and Dad divorced, and Dot began making her annual winter pilgrimage out of the New Jersey slush to my mother's sunny Southern California home.

"Dot was the last person left alive who ever saw me shoot," Mom said wistfully.

That isn't true, really — my sister and I spent most of the summer weekends of our childhoods watching Mom and Dad trapshooting, and we were even there a few of the many times that Mom won ribbons and trophies. But I was only seven or eight at the time, and my sister even younger, so we don't count. And Dad had gone on to a new life and was a little creeped out by the idea of reminiscing with an ex-wife he'd divorced three decades before, so he didn't count, either.

What Mom meant, I think, was that Dot was the person who remembered her at a time when her marriage hadn't yet turned sour, when her children were still young and unquestioning, when she could inhale a Jungle-Red-kissed Pall Mall with sensual gusto.

In the last twenty years of Mom's life, she won awards for her work as a marriage and family therapist, saved countless relationships, was beloved by her clients and colleagues alike. She married Allan, a tall broad-shouldered bicyclist a decade younger than she, who adored her and let her boss him around as much as she wanted. When her disease made it too difficult for her to see clients anymore, she turned her attention to writing, teaching creative writing classes for senior citizens and publishing several short articles about issues in relationship counseling.

But none of that apparently felt like her essential self. Unless you saw her when she was raven-haired, red-lipped, squinting into the sun, shouting "Pull" and taking aim and firing as the clay pigeon exploded into yellow powder against the blue sky, you didn't really know her. And fat old Dot, bitching away in her smoker's croak while Mom coughed and coughed and coughed, was the only one left to help hold that memory.

+ + +

During the year or two after my marriage ended, I was doing a lot of experimenting. Frank and I had failed to figure out how I could become an adept sadomasochist while he enjoyed his mostly vanilla sexuality, and we had decided to call it quits — but it's one thing to know that you're a big pervert at heart, and another thing altogether to figure out how to play and how to find people to play with, particularly in a small city like Sacramento in the 1980s. In the meantime, I was pretty much fucking everyone, and sneaking a little kink in when I could wheedle their permission.

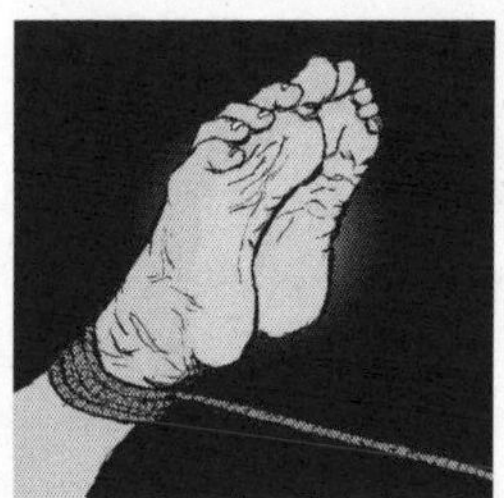

I met Jim through our mutual friend and lover, Sharon. I'd been playing with Sharon for a while — she was my first female partner — but our sex life together had never quite clicked for me: Although she was willing to indulge my kinky desires, the only one that really lit her up was being bound. I didn't mind tying her, but if I wasn't going to get to hurt her I couldn't really see the point in it. (I have an extensive history with partners who love to be tied up, and my feelings about that haven't changed in the intervening three decades.) Sensing that my interest was waning, she'd started bringing me men like a cat brings in half-killed birds. Jim was the first but not the last.

Although he was around my height — 5'4" — Jim was a former construction worker and was built like a cinder block. Unlike Frank, who is also short and strong, Jim was unafraid to use his strength in bed, tossing me around like a rag doll; his penis, as girthy as its owner, was attention-getting as well. At that point I considered myself exclusively a top, so I was startled by what a turn-on it was to be quite literally manhandled: He never hurt me, but being overpowered — it might be more accurate to say being overpowerable — was an altogether new thrill. (And I wonder, to be honest, if I'd have been as comfortable with that sort of play with Frank, with whom I'd shared my life. I had and have a huge need to be in charge of my world, so there is much to be said for being able to walk away from being overpowerable when the scene is over.)

Jim was a particular subtype of heterosexual male douche that I'm sure you've encountered: boastful and insecure, constantly struggling with money, dating woman after woman but not actually seeming to like us much. He had no interest at all in doing kink with me, although I suspect he might have sung a different tune if I had been willing to bottom. Even as commonplace an activity as light biting or scratching was completely verboten.

He was, however, endlessly fascinated with hearing the stories I was bringing back from my increasingly creative and enlightening adventures, and never tired of teasing me about my predilections. At one point he produced a battered old singletail whip he'd found somewhere, the kind people buy to be Indiana Jones for Halloween, and expected me to greet it with delight — at that point in my journey I had never so much as touched a singletail, but even I knew that the stiff dusty relic was unsuitable for anything but a tacky wall decoration.

But I was new to kink and new to singlehood, and operating under the belief that Sacramento had few to no men who matched my kinks and personality. (It's common for novice pervs to believe that they are the only one in the world who wants what they want, and thus to be a bit less selective than safety or enjoyment would dictate.) I fucked Jim off and on for a year or two, until one night he called me after quite a few drinks to blame me angrily for a woman who, he said, refused to date him because he hung out with lowlifes like me. It might even have been true. Regardless, it pissed me off enough that I never saw Jim again.

Sharon and I have stayed friends for more than three decades, though. I remember a conversation from around that time, in which we were comparing notes about the best lover we'd ever had.

I sighed. "I hate to admit it, but I think it was Jim."

She shot me a startled look. "Fuck, me too." We looked at each other for a long moment. "But I don't *want* it to be Jim!"

I didn't either, but it was. The endless struggle between nice-guy and sexy-beast had scored yet another point in the wrong column.

+++

A few years back, Sharon sent me a copy of Jim's obituary: He had died after "a brief illness," all of fifty-eight years old. He was the first lover of mine, as far as I know, to die.

That part of my life — when I was figuring out how to be a single woman, how to be a divorced parent, how to be a sadomasochist, how to make a living as a freelance writer — is dimming in my mind; after all, it's been more than three decades, hundreds of lovers and play partners, a dozen books, a dozen homes in half a dozen cities. At least two of the people I was fucking back then have died since Jim, and I've lost track of all the rest, except Sharon. Even now, as I write my memories, I'm not sure how much is completely true — was it Jim who gave me the whip, or his friend Pete?

Will that Janet, the one who fucks people in the vain hope that one of them will let her spank them, the one who listens obsessively to the cast album of *Chess* to try to draw some meaning from its story about leaving one man and finding another, the one who bears only the slightest resemblance to the Janet who is writing this — will she still exist when Sharon is gone?

If I end up the last one standing, what will be left of me?

9. On Loss

Losing, — one thing or person after another — is part of aging. Part of aging *well* is recognizing the things you get back.

I suppose I lost my umbilical cord at some point, although I don't remember that. It was the last bit of a previous existence, the one where I floated in a warm, quiet place, outside time, outside space. Losing it meant gaining myself: I had become an individual, charging forward into my life in this body, for better or for worse.

I do have a vague recollection of losing my baby teeth. Because I was little and impatient, I gained a quarter every time — but what I really gained, some months later, were bigger, better teeth.

Of course, those don't last forever either. The mouth surgery required pulling six teeth to prepare my jaws for repositioning. With the previous loss of my wisdom teeth, and the subsequent loss of two molars that were causing problems, I'm now down to twenty teeth, same as your five-year-old niece — make of that what you will. I spent two years wearing braces and two months with my teeth wired shut, but at the end I had a nice, even bite and an actual chin, which was not something I'd had until that point.

Now, of course, I have several of them.

+ + +

And then there was my virginity. Like my baby teeth, I was in a hurry to get rid of it; unlike my baby teeth, losing it was neither easy nor natural. First, there was the struggle to find a willing second. For a plump, know-it-all-ish, and generally weird young woman (with a tendency to attract and be attracted to young men who were on the verge of coming out as gay), that part took several years, and lasted till the summer after high school graduation.

I learned after several attempts that nature had gifted me with an unusually tough hymen. I ended up at my university's student clinic, where a doctor removed the offending membrane with a scalpel. Of course, by then the previous attempts had left me with a bout of vaginismus (for the non-vulva-bearing reader, this is a syndrome in which anxiety tightens the vagina enough to make penetration painful) that persisted for a couple of years. However, I had gained the ability to have sex — although not the ability to have good sex; that came much later, after I became an active pervert.

Is getting your period a gain or a loss? I guess I simultaneously gained the ability to have children — of all my life accomplishments, Miles and Ben are the ones of which I'm proudest — and lost several days of comfortable freedom every month. By my mid-fifties I was calling myself "Our Lady of Perpetual Menstruation," so I chose to have an endometrial ablation. That choice bracketed my reproductive life with medical interventions: the hymen removal at the beginning, the endometrium removal at the end. I waited a while to feel a sense of loss about menstruating, but it's been nearly two decades and that particular sadness has never shown up for as much as a moment.

+ + +

Change is, of course, inevitable, but I find that I do best when I refuse to frame it as either a loss or a gain. Change just *is,* and my attempts to control it or ignore it rarely end well for me or anyone else.

My love life has changed often over the last half century or so — from hetero to bi, from monogamous to anything-but, from vanilla to kinky, from abundant to abstemious. But whatever kinds of sex and love I might have been having at the time, I've never quite understood the meaning of the word "romance." This confusion, as you can imagine, is sometimes an obstacle for someone who writes about all the different ways people can construct their relationships.

Of course, I'm not immune to the cultural frenzy to achieve romantic love — I saw the same movies that everyone else did. But I guess I never really thought they applied to me. My first marriage was to a great friend, and once we were done trying to be married, we got to be great friends again. My second long-term coupling was the closest I've ever come to a romantic relationship, which is to say that the sex was awesome and that we were poorly suited in almost every other way. And you've already heard about Edward and me. I've had a lot of other relationships along the way, ranging from casual to devoted to incendiary, but none of them have felt particularly romantic to me.

Another thing that has changed a lot, of course, is the cast of characters, the people I know and care about: This is planet Earth, and, like Oz, "people come and go so quickly here." But the word "grief" confuses me too; it seems like "romance" is the word one is supposed to use for gaining someone, and "grief" for losing them, and that seems to me like a vast oversimplification.

I've lost a lot of people who have been important to me, and a few I've loved deeply. But when I hear folks talk about grieving, it seems to me that it's more than just missing someone. It sounds like it's about being sad.

When someone escapes physical or emotional pain by dying, any sadness I feel is more for me than for them. They won't be there anymore to chat with or buy gifts for or hug, and that sucks — but the way I see it, my sadness is far less important than their comfort and agency.

It might be different if my loved ones were in the habit of departing the mortal plane before they'd lived a full life. (I am unspeakably lucky, for example, that nobody I love has ever been lost to assault or similar violence.) And the idea that anyone I care about might have to buy their return ticket to the Great Whatever using the currency of suffering — that infuriates me. But the folks I've loved were mostly ready to go by the time they left, and I've felt happy for them that they got to leave on their own terms — before things got too bad.

+++

I do feel sad, sometimes intolerably, *before* someone dies. It doesn't last long, and I recover quickly. But while it lasts, it feels like all my guts are being yanked out through my eyes.

+++

Over dinner, I said, "Boy, did you see those new photos of Ruthie? She looks like she's ready to pop any moment. Twins, can you imagine what that must feel like?"

"God, yes," Mom agreed. "I wish ... " She began to cough, and we waited politely for it to stop. She liked it best if we pretended the coughing wasn't happening; if you were talking when the coughing began, you were supposed to go on talking. But she was the one who was talking, so Allan and I went on eating our meat loaf as calmly as we could until she recovered, " ... I was going to be here to see them."

"Well, you probably will," I said, diplomatically.

Allan applied himself busily to his peas.

"Oh ... didn't I tell you? I've set a date."

She knew she hadn't told me; she was bluffing on that part. However, if Mom had set a date, there was no arguing with her. I swallowed my food with difficulty and made a neutrally interrogative sound.

"Yeah, about six weeks from now. I was going to do it sooner, but your sister is going to be out of the country, and she asked me to wait until she gets back."

Part of me had been waiting to hear this conversation for several months, agreed with it, was proud of her for living up to her lifelong intention, which I share. A bigger part of me was beyond reasoning or speech, a raw insensate howl. I waited for the meal to end, helped carry the dishes to the kitchen, excused myself, retreated to the spare room, and fell apart: horrible, racking, choking sobs made even more painful by my successful attempt to keep them silent.

I clogged the howl with the package of meringues I'd bought to fortify me for a visit to my dying mother, and rejoined Mom and Allan in front of the TV.

+++

The evening came when my dog Amy, my best girl, my heart-dog, could no longer climb the steps to sleep next to my side of the bed the way she had for more than a decade. Edward and I got her upstairs using a folded towel under her belly to support her hips, but we'd decided beforehand that "not being able to climb the stairs by herself" was our bright, clear line that meant she was in too much pain to be alive anymore.

The next morning, I called the vet who made that kind of house call. "Hi," I said, "this is Janet. We've decided that it's Amy's time...." and then suddenly I couldn't breathe because I was crying too hard. Edward gently took the phone away from me and finished the conversation with the vet.

Yet ten minutes later, when the front doorbell rang and it was the guy from the utility company needing help to find the meter, I doubt he could tell that I'd been crying: the tears were wretched, painful sobs, but they only lasted a couple of minutes, and then I was back to my usual, pragmatic self.

+++

Attending a death is a different matter. After Amy, and then Mom, and then Dad, had died, I mostly felt like I needed a stiff drink. Being with someone who is dying is harrowing. (So, for the record, is being with someone who is giving birth. A story for another time.)

I think of them, and many more people I've loved, almost every day. There's a dog a few blocks from here who at first glance looks like Amy, which means looking like a discarded roll of charcoal-gray shag carpeting with legs. When I pass that dog out for a walk with its owner, my eyes get misty. And Mom loved earrings that covered the sagging holes in her ears, but were still dangly (not all that easy to find), and every time I see a pair I have to remind myself not to buy them for her.

But do I grieve the ones I've lost? I don't think so. I miss them, but I don't grieve them: They were ready to go, and they went. It would be much sadder if they'd had to go on suffering.

+++

Sometimes I feel like I'm broken, not being able to understand romance, not being able to understand grief. But here's the only definition of "love" that makes any sense to me, and it helps answer the question of why I don't understand.

The voices of certain people live permanently inside my head. Some are alive, some are not. If I want to know what my ex-husband thinks about something, I can ask the Frank who lives in my brain. (The physical Frank is still alive, but a major stroke left him struggling to communicate his thoughts — although they're as sensible and amusing as ever, if you can figure out what he's trying to say.) Likewise, my friend Paul, who is still alive but is five hundred miles away, or my frequent coauthor Dossie, who is the same. And one of the biggest emotional glitches I encountered when contemplating top surgery was seeing the expression on my father's face upon learning that I was planning to spend a chunk of the money he left me to get my tits cut off.

None of those loves are, or were, what I'd call "romantic." And I can't feel grief for the loved ones who are gone, because they're not — they're right here between my ears.

+++

Perhaps at the moment of dying, you stop — you cease. And then you de-cease, becoming something else that we cannot begin to imagine. Being de-ceased doesn't sound like too bad a deal to me.

+++

One of the things I figured out during my various journeys into physical and emotional extremes is that our bodies force us to live in time and space — that's what bodies are for. However, I've taken a couple of trips out of my body for a millisecond or two, and gotten to see that other existence, the one outside time and space where everyone goes when they've lost their bodies and nothing glues them in place anymore.

I've come to think of my lifetime as a relatively brief vacation, and my body as resortwear — perhaps a nice sundress, or a pair of comfy shorts. Like all vacations, this one will feel like it's over much too soon. And also like all vacations, I will return to my real existence with a handful of nice memories and a certain sense of relief about leaving all that rigmarole behind me.

Trying to imagine existence outside time and space does for your brain what planks do for your abs, times a couple of thousand. But it seems clear to me that Mom and Dad and Amy and the rest are both everywhere and nowhere, at all times and at no time. Which means that the Mom and Dad and Amy who live in my brain are the same as the Mom and Dad and Amy whose vacations are over (and, for that matter, the Mom and Dad and Amy whose company I enjoyed for all those years).

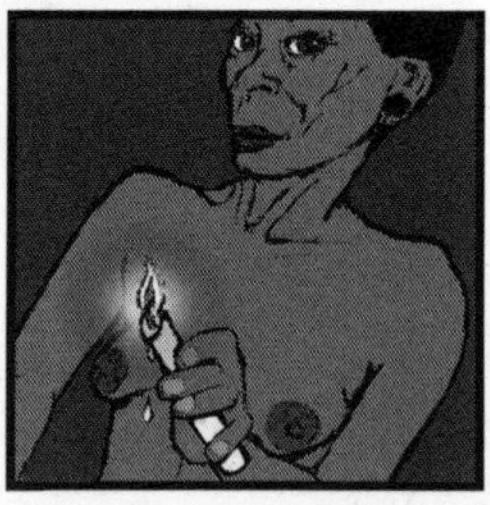

To paraphrase Dan Hicks, who has also left his body behind — How can I miss them when they won't go away?

10. On Transitions

Edward and I didn't move to Oregon because of its right-to-die laws, but we're glad to have them. In a chat with the staff of the retirement community we're expecting to move to, we asked what happens with their residents who have decided it's time to go. We were delighted to learn that the community not only supports that decision but has a death doula on staff. Holding the hand of someone you love as they leave their body is something nobody should have to do alone.

+++

Here's the thing about getting married at fifty-five (him) and fifty (me): the vow about "till death do us part" gets all too real. When you stand in the Alameda County Courthouse and say those words, you're acknowledging that each of you will help the other through the indignities and travails of living in an aging body, and that one of you will someday watch the other one die.

I once saw an article in a suburban paper headlined "Tragic Death of Local Couple." I read on and learned that the pair — him in his eighties, her in her seventies — had chartered a fishing boat and were sailing around the Caribbean, when the boat capsized, and they both drowned.

If that's a "tragic death," sign me up. Dying while doing what you love best, and not having to watch the person you love suffer and dwindle, sounds to me like an excellent way to go. (I have no way of knowing for sure, of course, but I'd bet a few bucks that their death was completely intentional, and I bow to their courage in making that choice.)

+ + +

My father was always the toughest person on my Christmas list; he didn't want much, and when he did want something, he bought it. So I fell into a ritual: Each year, I packed up a box of jams, cookies, fruitcake and other homemade goodies (with extra gingersnaps, which he loved), and added a copy of whatever book I'd most enjoyed in the preceding year.

The book I most enjoyed in 2018 was George Saunders's *Lincoln in the Bardo* — but as a gift for a dying man, the story of the lost souls in the graveyard of Lincoln's son seemed tactless. So instead, I bought him the ebook of Neil Gaiman and Terry Pratchett's wonderful *Good Omens,* because I figured he could use a good laugh and I couldn't imagine anyone not loving *Good Omens.*

In the days after Dad's death, I was packing up a few things to take home with me. I picked up his Kindle, thinking Miles or Ben might want it, and looked to see what he had been reading.

He was only a third of the way through *Good Omens.*

That's sad.

Death interrupts such small pleasures: the end of *Good Omens,* the next episode of *Masterpiece Theatre,* the tickets to the big game. To choose death, as he did, means that these little expectations have been outweighed by a bigger consideration: for the depressed, the inability to take joy in such temporary pleasures; for the sick, the specter of enough pain to outweigh the joy.

For Dad, I think it was a little of each. His beloved wife Mona had died the previous summer — aside from a few short hospital stays, the two of them had never spent a night apart in their thirty-four years of marriage. Mona was ten years his junior, so he had never imagined outliving her, until she died of cancer just a few weeks after her diagnosis.

There's no way to describe what happened next without resorting to cliché: the spark went out of his eye, the lift out of his step, all the ways we try to describe the sudden shrinkage of a soul. When Mona died, Dad became old overnight. His Parkinson's flared and overwhelmed the medicine that had controlled it, he stopped taking pleasure in food or books or television. I think receiving his own cancer diagnosis a few months later was almost a relief. The doctor said they'd caught it soon enough that chemo and surgery stood a pretty good chance of success, but Dad was old by then, and all that sounded like way too much trouble.

I think those of us who are fortunate enough to live past sixty or so will eventually hit such a tipping point — the point where you're past all the clichés about "still feeling seventeen," "an oldie but a goodie," references to fine wine, and so on, and suddenly you're just plain old.

If you've ever been close to someone who made that transition, it's unmistakable: the caution, the fragility, the resignation. The trigger is sometimes a health crisis, sometimes the death of a beloved, sometimes the loss of a familiar and comfortable job or art or hobby, and sometimes just a gradual decline that has become a bit steeper than a person can keep up with.

The change is often accompanied by depression, but that one's tough to call. If you look at a standard depression checklist, the criteria include hopelessness, sleep problems, loss of interest in previously engaging things, and so on. If you're in chronic pain, if mortality is bearing down on you, if you've lost abilities that used to delight you — well, it's hard to argue against that being depression. But another description for it is "old age."

+++

I haven't hit that moment yet when it comes to old age. But when I was in my forties, I marched in the San Francisco Pride Parade directly behind the White Rat Morris Dancers, who bill themselves as "the world's first queer / pervert / leather Morris dance troupe" (with a modest "as far as we know"). The White Rats observe many of the traditions of British Morris dancing, with hankies and sticks and bells, only their bells are sewn onto the skin of their upper arms with monofilament line threaded through temporary piercings.

For some reason nobody has ever figured out, the "cool gray city of love" always becomes the "hot sunny city of sweat" just in time for Pride. I was in a schoolmarm outfit that year — long leather skirt, white blouse buttoned to the neck, necktie, hair slicked back, a rattan cane in my hand — and I was parboiling. And while I didn't envy the Rats having to dance down the entire mile and a half parade route in that heat, I really envied them those piercings, because in my experience, play piercings are the cheapest endorphins in the world:

a brief sting that settles into a low pleasant ache as the piercee gently lifts off the ground and floats overhead.

By the next year, being the problem-solver I am, I'd figured out the best of both worlds. My Pride outfit that year and thereafter was a pair of green suede chaps worn over a black thong, with matching green suede pasties sewn on to cover my nipples — which made for a startling suntan, and was a lot of fun. For the first year or two, a deft friend did my piercings for me, and my happy, high self enjoyed every step of those parades.

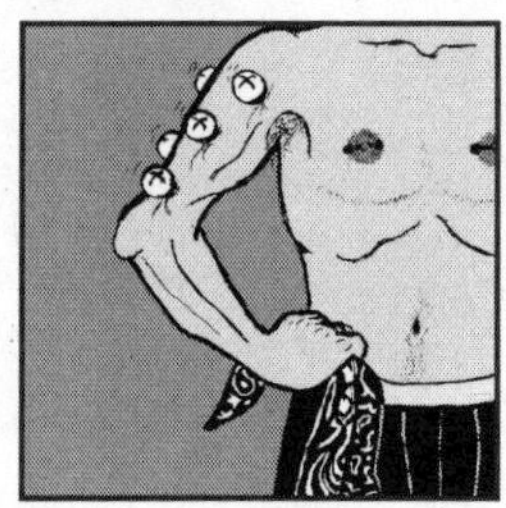

But then there came a year when my friend was not available, and I decided to do my own piercings. I set myself up in the bathroom, with needles and monofilament and alcohol and pasties. I tried to do the first piercing, and discovered to my annoyance that while my nipples were a lot farther from my eyes than they'd once been, they were still too near for me to see clearly. I capped the contaminated needle and slammed it into the trash, stomped out of the bathroom, and got my reading glasses from my nightstand, muttering "I'm getting too fucking old for this shit" the whole way.

At that point I gave up trying to think of myself as anything but middle-aged. I'm still awaiting the epiphany that tips me over into feeling old.

+ + +

For me, the best way to imagine death is as the mirror image of birth: a transition from one state of being to another. In his novel *Evening Star,* Larry McMurtry describes an infant's encounter with a dying woman: "When [the baby] looked into her eyes, with his nose almost touching her face, he suddenly thought he saw the Other Place.... He tried to remember the Other Place, but he couldn't."

In that framework, becoming old could be viewed as transition labor — preparation for the hard work of being pushed into the next existence.

Once in a while, you see a friend fall into that torpor — and, against all odds, make it back out. My beloved Dossie has done this a couple of times: Her spine is doing its best to collapse like a concertina, which means a whole lot of pain, then a major surgery, then more pain and a long recovery. When I talk to her during all that, she is old. But when the recovery is over and she can hike again — hiking is her path to sanity, a connection a sedentary person like me can recognize but cannot possibly understand — she's back to being Dossie again, full of plans and ideas and hopes.

That "old" state of mind does not necessarily track to chronological age. One acquaintance of mine was still working as a professional dominatrix at eighty — that was nearly twenty years ago. (I asked for, and received, permission to grow up to be her, and I'm doing my best.) I recently re-encountered her on Facebook, and she seems to be the same buoyant spirit she's always been.

And just last week, I was taking out the garbage and my next-door neighbor Mel was out, stumping along with his walker, with his little dog Rusty surging eagerly ahead. I asked him how he was doing, and he said, jovially, "Still walking!" Mel turned 101 a month or two back — almost exactly half again my age. Which gave me considerable pause about my authority to write a book about aging, but, well, here we are.

Edward has been old for a few years now, and that's not easy on either of us. I am pushing back against aging, but I have some advantages: I still have a reasonable number of pain-free days, and work that keeps me connected to friends and readers all over the globe, plus a deeply ingrained need for independence and a generally ornery disposition that is disinclined to listen to any whisperings about what someone like me is "supposed to" be doing.

He, on the other hand, seems to have resigned himself to the downward slide. He relinquished his driver's license a couple of years ago, and does no travel that takes more than an hour or two. He does not like to be left alone overnight because he sometimes falls. And, in theory, I knew all this was coming when I married him — I used to tell friends that I was living their future for them. But I didn't expect it to happen so soon, or so thoroughly, or so one-sidedly.

Statistically, he has a fair chance of outliving me, despite the difference in our ages. But, hell, I'm not even seventy. One of these days my Geezer Card will arrive in the mail (it's not the same as an AARP card; I already have one of those), but I'm hoping not to have to open the envelope just yet.

11. On the End

My friend Andrew stopped getting older yesterday.

I suppose you could think of death as the ultimate safeword: When life gets too painful or strenuous or awful, the body or the spirit can stop the scene. (Which is why laws against suicide, and against assisted suicide, are very bad models of consent. Any top who ignores a safeword will find themselves persona non grata in their local scene, and rightly so — and what are those laws but ways to ignore a safeword?)

Andrew, as far as I know, was exclusively a top, but I feel certain that if he'd ever bottomed, he would have been one of those stubborn bottoms that will let a trusted top peel their skin off their bodies before they withdraw consent by safewording. Given that I was one of those bottoms myself, he and I always understood each other in the dungeon.

(A scene: We are at a play party. I am lying on a table made from a large, padded cable spool. He is alternating between caning me, a sensation I love, and biting my thighs, a sensation I hate. Neither of us wants bondage because we both like it when I fight back, which creates a dilemma: If he pushes me as far as we both want him to, there's a significant chance that I'll attack him physically. He's a strong guy, but I'm no pushover either, and one or both of us could get hurt in a scenario like that. So, with no discussion, we evolve a safe signal: As he savages me with his teeth, I tuck one hand into the back pocket of his jeans. The moment I withdraw it, he stops what he is doing to check in.)

And yet Andrew, beset by a cascade of medical problems that started with a cancer diagnosis and snowballed from there, safeworded

Andrew

out of life. The week before, he'd been enjoying a European vacation with his wife of many years, Paula — not the kind of adventure I'd expect anyone to undertake while being treated for cancer, but Andrew was an adventurer by nature: optimistic, energetic and certain of his own abilities. I don't think he ever really believed that he would die until the event was imminent — his last message to his friends, written a couple of days before his death, was cheerful and confident.

British-born Andrew was one of the best-read and best-educated folks in our circle, and had interesting things to say on pretty much any topic that came up. His and Paula's home was full of good things to read (staying in their guest room one night, I was delighted to find shelves full of paperbacks by P.G. Wodehouse, Dorothy Sayers and Terry Pratchett), good music to listen to, charming kids who have grown into charming adults, and good, unfussy food to eat. He and Paula were a well-matched team: Introverted Paula has a great gift for creating a warmly welcoming home, and extroverted Andrew drew friends from his many circles of interest: circus arts (he was an accomplished juggler and whip-cracker), BDSM, tech, and more.

Andrew and I were similar in our blithe belief in our own competence. He was born exactly ten days after I was. And until a few weeks ago, we were both operating under the assumption that we had decades of scenes to go before either of us would have to safeword out.

+++

I'm not much of a crier at the movies or theatre — I may dab at a little moisture, but I can count on one hand the number of times I've dissolved into a full-on, snotty, face-knotted-up, ugly cry. And nearly all of them have happened when I'm seeing what I call a "good death."

Of course, a lot of such deaths are due to "movie disease" — that desirable ailment that leaves its victim fresh-faced (except for perhaps a bit of dark Max Factor under the eyes and cheekbones, plus a dab of pale, matte lipstick), coherent, and with plenty of time to say their perfect goodbyes to the people they love. But even when I know I'm being played, the tears I'm shedding are the tears of my old friend, catharsis, otherwise known as joy. The person on screen is dying exactly as I hope to die, borne up by the occupants of their heart, with minimal discomfort and maximum love.

Few these days get to have that good death. I was in my mid-fifties by the time I saw a dead body (my mother's) — small wonder that most of us are so deeply uncomfortable with the idea of death that we're willing to do almost anything to postpone it for ourselves and those we care about, including allowing our lives to be prolonged into miserable absurdity.

I sometimes encounter friends who are wringing their hands over when to euthanize an ailing pet. Sometimes their decision seems to hinge on their own feelings and not those of the suffering animal. I find that hesitation difficult to forgive, though very easy to understand.

I wish it were as easy to help our friends and relatives die as it is our pets, but there are significant obstacles even in states like the one I call home, and most states don't allow assisted suicide at all. Nonetheless, people have been end-running the laws for decades — a lot of folks who were queer and living in a major city in the AIDS era spent a night or two attending bon voyage parties — and will always do so, because dying is tough enough without being forced to earn it with months or years of suffering.

I think it would be easier to see a loved one die if there were some physical manifestation that let us watch them gradually leaving one plane of existence and entering another. Perhaps their body could grow less and less opaque, like a movie ghost, until in the end they aren't there at all.

+++

Of course, this is a book about aging, not dying. But part of aging is packing for that final trip.

I believe that voyage is still far in the future, but then again, so did Andrew.

+++

Here are some things I'd like to do during my lifetime:

- See the aurora borealis.
- Bungee-jump.
- Fuck an uncircumcised man, without a condom, again. (The one time I did this was the only time in my life I've orgasmed from plain old missionary intercourse. I'd love to know if that was a fluke or if it happens every time.)
- Write a musical.

- Own a gigantic dog.
- Visit Africa.
- Visit Asia.
- Try psychedelics.
- Enroll in another MFA program. Or, better yet, spend the rest of my life bouncing from one MFA program to the next.
- Live in a high-rise apartment.
- Learn to play a musical instrument.
- Learn another language.
- Learn to paint portraits in oils.
- Fist someone anally.
- Surf.

Being the age I am means recognizing that I will not get to do a lot of these things. Gigantic dogs are not particularly safe pets for fragile elders, and besides, I can't see having one in a senior apartment. Bungee-jumping looks like huge flying fun and also like an excellent way to fuck up an aging back. I don't think most MFA programs are open to sequential enrollment over a period of decades. By the time I get my long-undisturbed vagina ready to accept a penis, its owner will probably have wandered off in search of damper pastures. And so on.

But look at what I *have* done. I've written books, and I'm proud of nearly all of them (and, no, I'm not telling which ones aren't included in that statement). I've raised two spectacular sons. I've maintained several decade-plus relationships. I ran a small business for nearly three decades — I wouldn't necessarily call it a *successful* small business, but somehow I kept the doors open and put food on the table. I've raised dozens of pets, cooked thousands of tasty meals, bought and decorated at least a dozen houses. I've been fat, and been less fat, and been strong under the fat whether there was lots or a little. I've traveled to new places, and embraced sad friends, and attended the dying, and helped bring a person into the world. I've been friends with amazing people, and, more to the point, they've been friends with me.

It may be that by the time this book sees print, I won't be here anymore — I'll have raced ahead of you in the journey back to spacelessness and timelessness. Or maybe you'll go first, and I won't get to meet you there just yet. But whichever order we go in, I'm hoping for a great death for everyone reading this: in physical and emotional comfort, surrounded by the bodies and spirits of those we love and who love us.

That's the brass ring dangling just outside the merry-go-round. It's the aftercare at the end of our long challenging scene, being held in the arms of a loving Something while we float gently away.

Bon voyage — to you and everyone else reading this. I'll see you soon.

Acknowledgements

This book would not exist without the support and love of:

Edward Goehring
Dossie Easton
Miles, Ben, Destiny and Felix Taber
Lisa Rogers
Patrick Mulcahey
Paul Romano
“Sharon”
The Conways
The Bergens
The brunch gang

My crack team of beta readers, especially Carly Dreyfus and Max Cameron

The memories of Dick Hardy and Susan Hardy

Our lovely four-footeds, Augie, Willow, Pearl and Nick

and Patrick Davis and his colleagues at Unbound Edition Press, including Avery Langston

as well as all the lovely aging perverts (and aren’t we all aging, and a little perverted?) who have inspired and inflamed me through the years

About the Author

Janet W. Hardy is the author or coauthor of more than a dozen groundbreaking books about relationships and sexuality, including *The Ethical Slut,* which has sold more than 500,000 copies to date and has been translated into more than a dozen languages.

She spent the first three decades of her life believing that she was the only person in the world who got turned on by thinking about spanking. She wrote her first book, *The Sexually Dominant Woman,* to help create a world in which nobody else would ever be that clueless.

Janet has traveled the world as a speaker and teacher on topics ranging from ethical multi-partner relationships to erotic spanking and beyond. She has appeared in documentary films, television shows, and more podcasts and radio shows than she can count. She has narrated audio versions of many of her books.

Janet spent a quarter century as editor-in-chief of Greenery Press, the firm she founded in 1992, which went on to publish dozens of books about alternative sexuality and relationships. While she has retired from publishing, she goes on writing, drawing, editing, speaking, and educating about sexuality.

Janet lives the life of a kinky poly queer genderbent geezer in Eugene, Oregon, with her equally kinky poly queer genderbent spouse.

About the Type and Paper

Designed by Malou Verlomme of the Monotype Studio, Macklin is an elegant, high-contrast typeface. It has been designed purposely for more emotional appeal.

The concept for Macklin began with research on historical material from Britain and Europe dating to the beginning of the 19th century, specifically the work of Vincent Figgins. Verlomme pays respect to Figgins's work with Macklin, but pushes the family to a more contemporary place.

This book is printed on natural Rolland Enviro Book stock. The paper is 100 percent post-consumer sustainable fiber content and is FSC-certified.

Notes of an Aging Pervert was designed by Eleanor Safe and Joseph Floresca.

Unbound Edition Press champions honest, original voices. Committed to the power of writers who explore and illuminate the contemporary human condition, we publish collections of poetry, short fiction, and essays. Our publisher and editorial team aim to identify, develop, and defend authors who create thoughtfully challenging work which may not find a home with mainstream publishers. We are guided by a mission to respect and elevate emerging, under-appreciated, and marginalized authors, with a strong commitment to advancing LGBTQ+ and BIPOC voices. We are honored to make meaningful contributions to the literary arts by publishing their work.

unboundedition.com